PAUL PFEIFFER

HERAUSGEGEBEN VON /
EDITED BY K21
KUNSTSAMMLUNG
NORDRHEIN-WESTFALEN

MIT TEXTEN VON / WITH TEXTS BY
STEFANO BASILICO
VALERIA LIEBERMANN
UND EINEM GESPRÄCH ZWISCHEN /
AND A CONVERSATION BETWEEN
PAUL PFEIFFER
& THOMAS RUFF

HATJE CANTZ

PAUL PFEIFFER

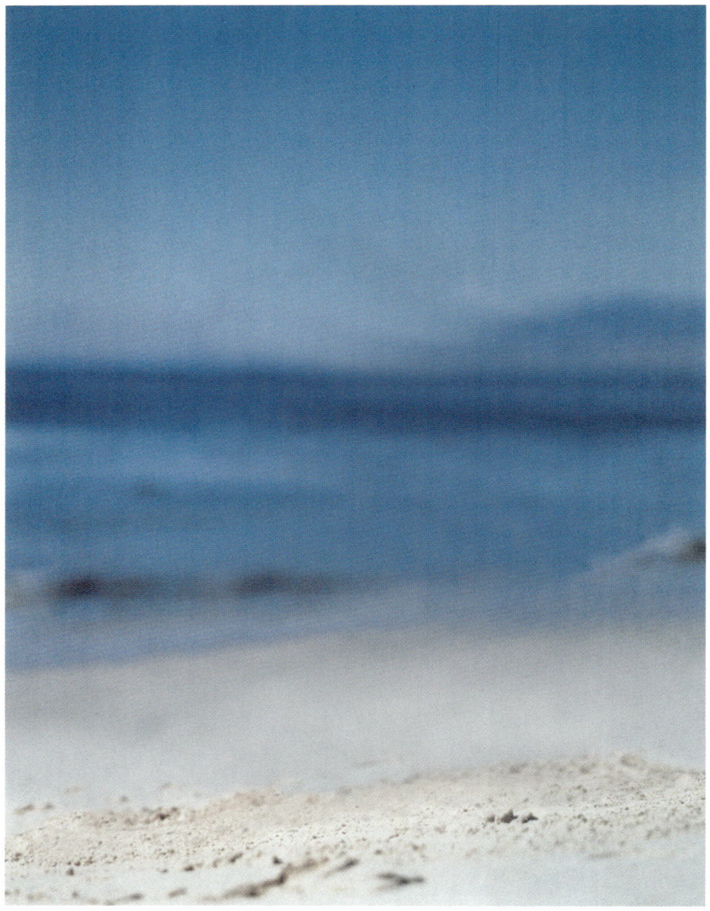

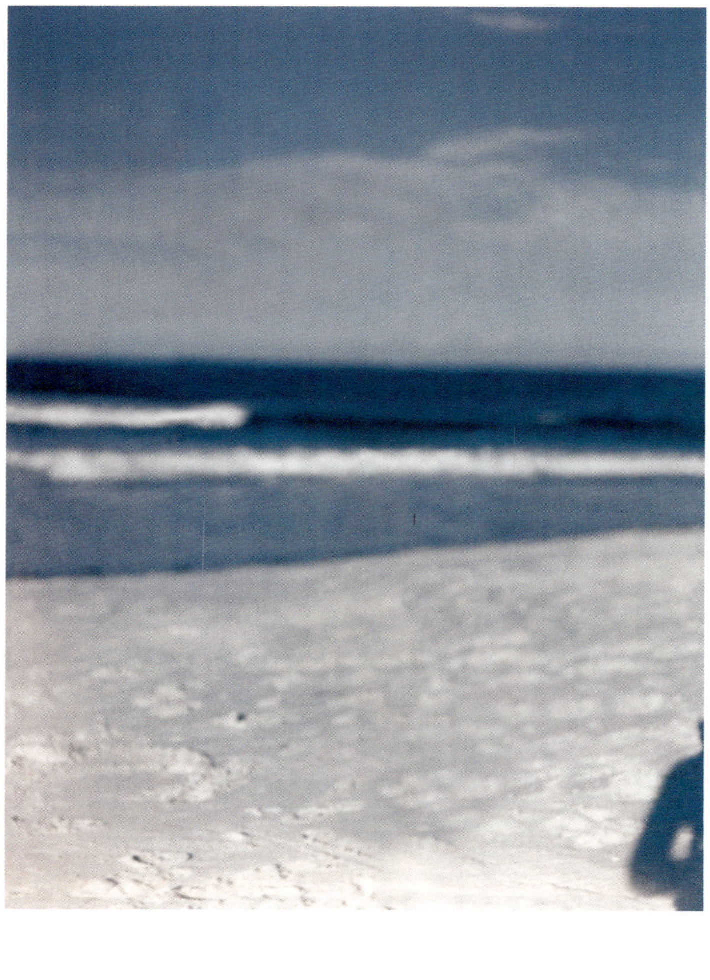

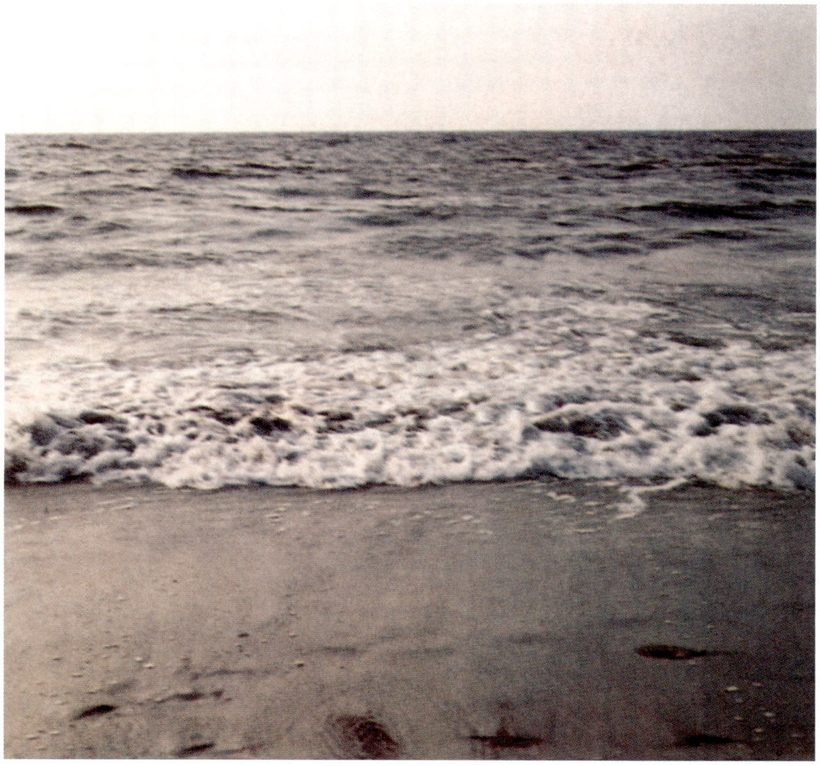

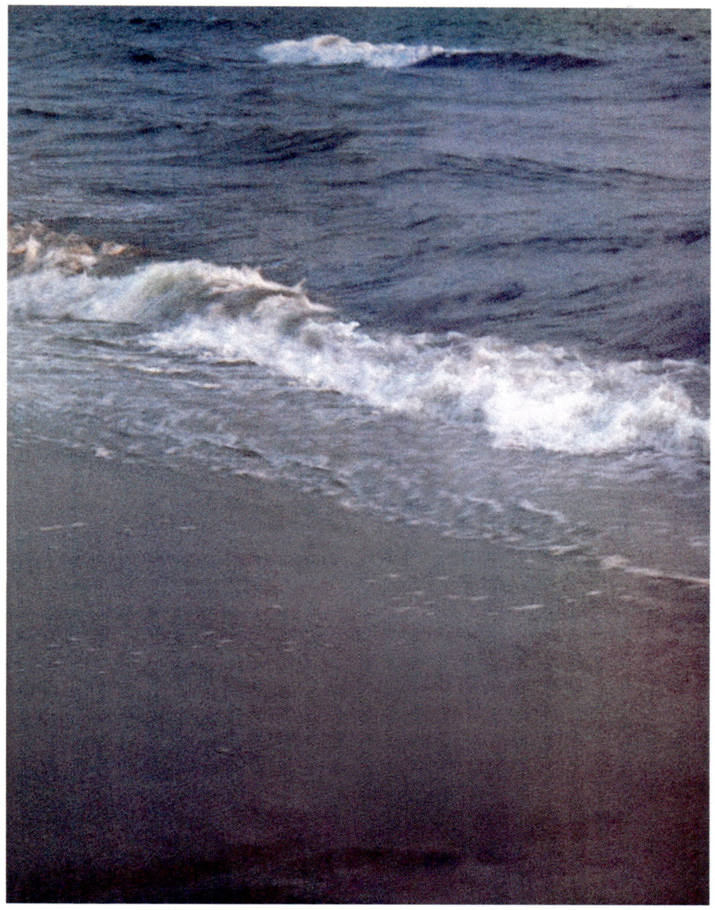

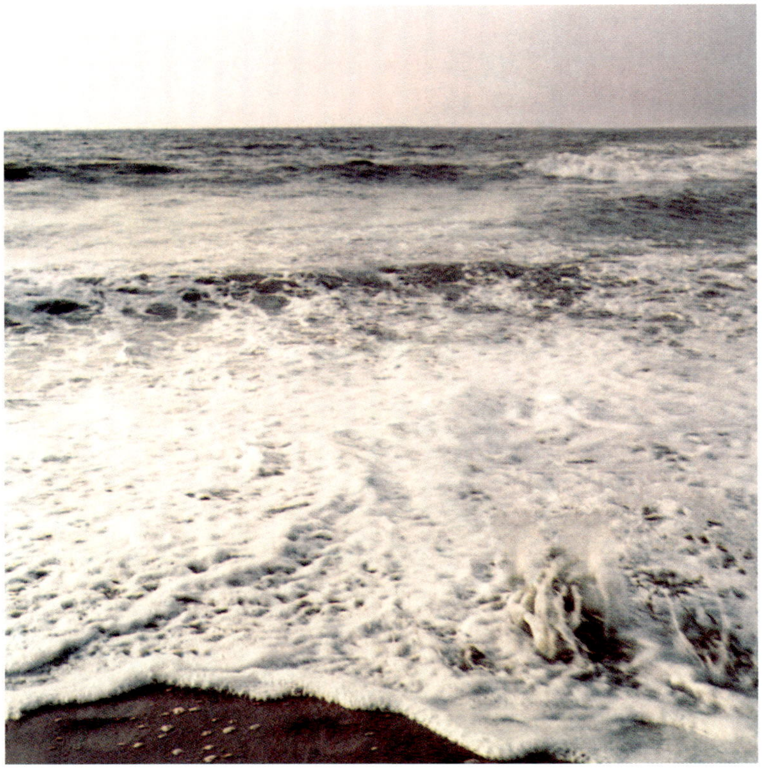

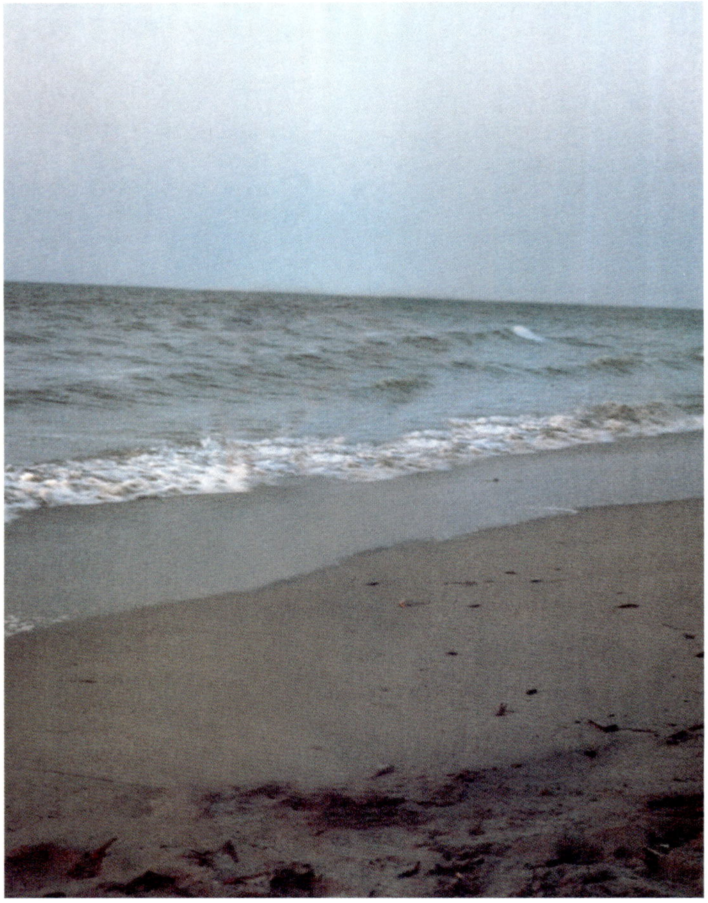

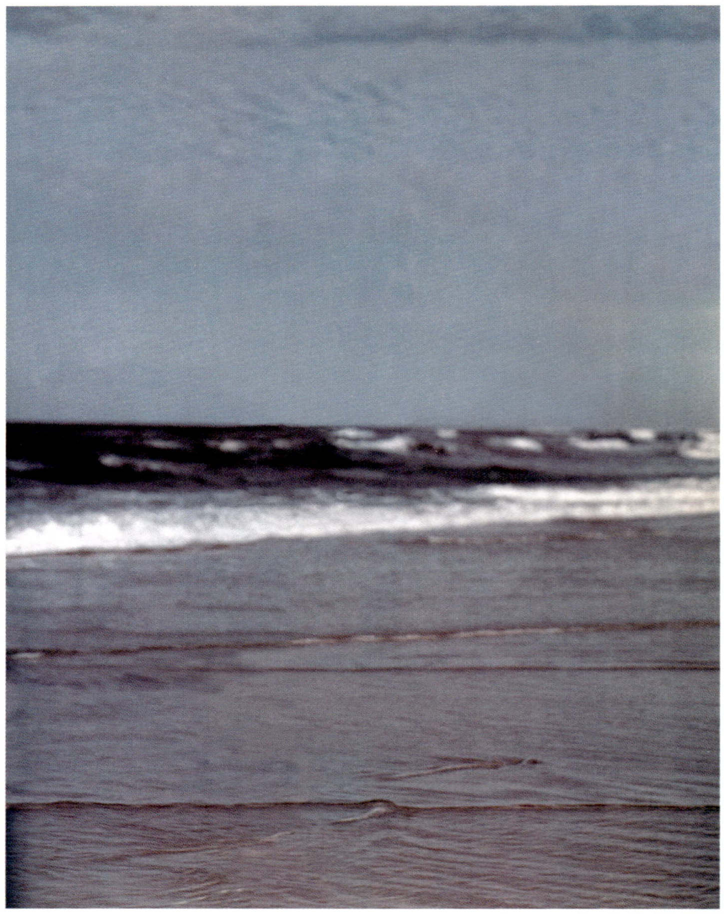

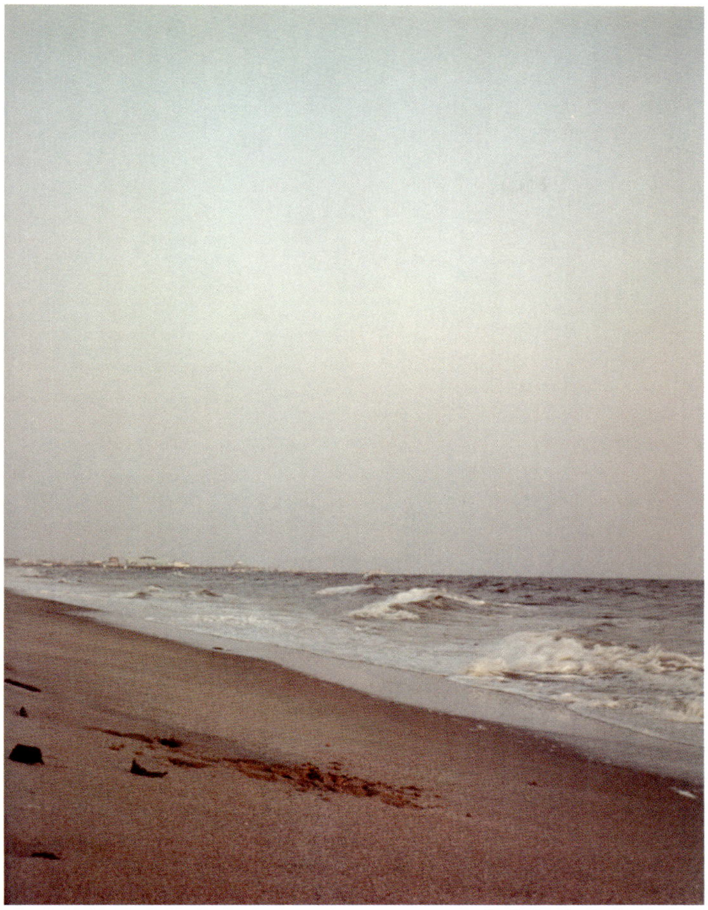

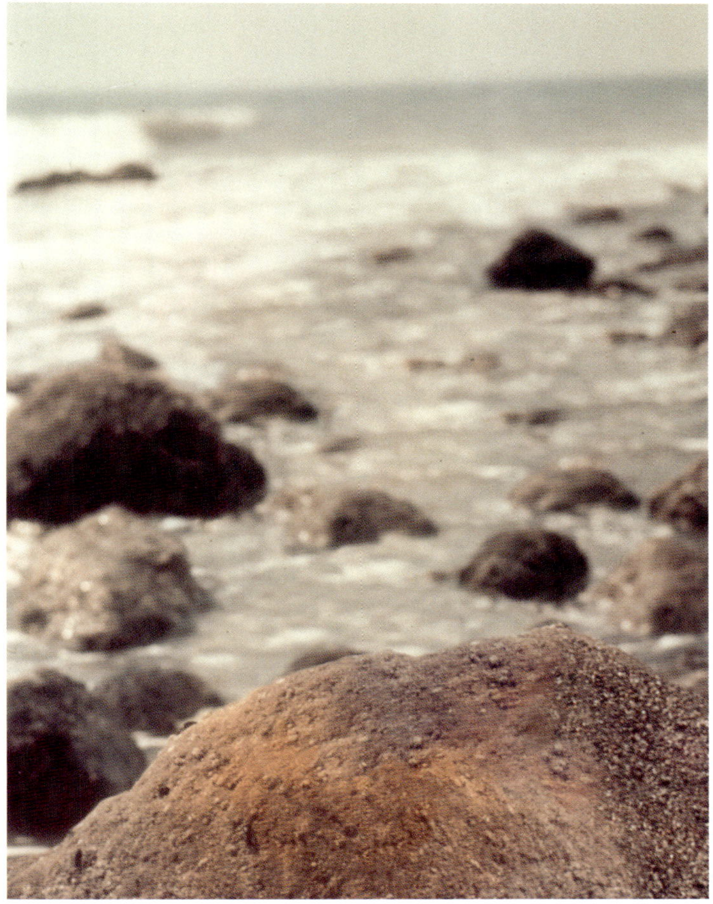

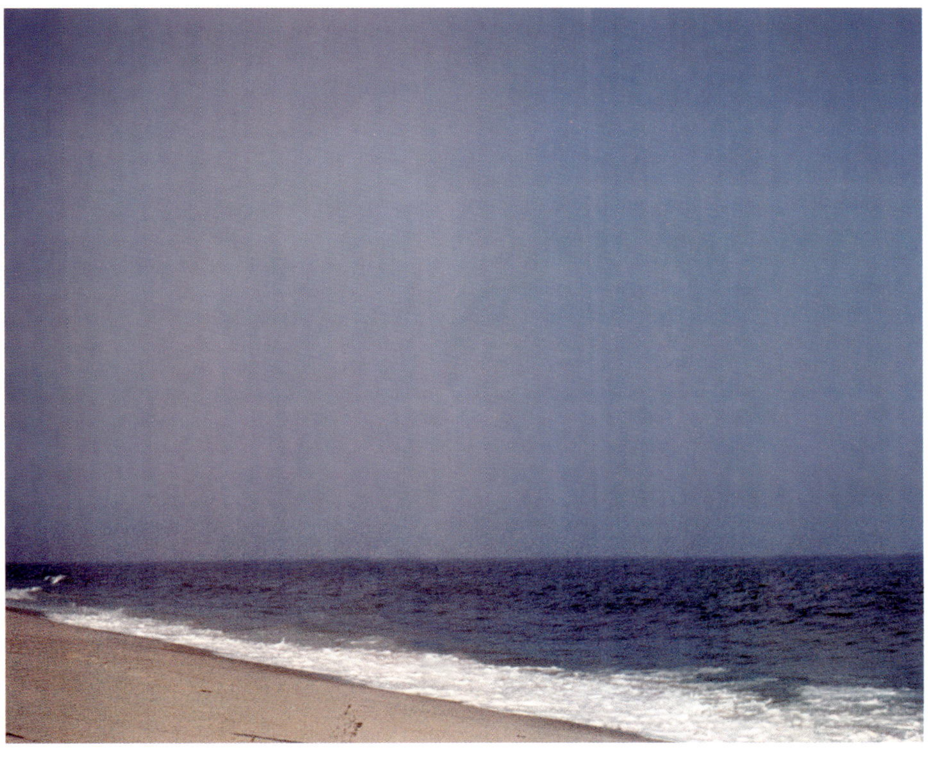

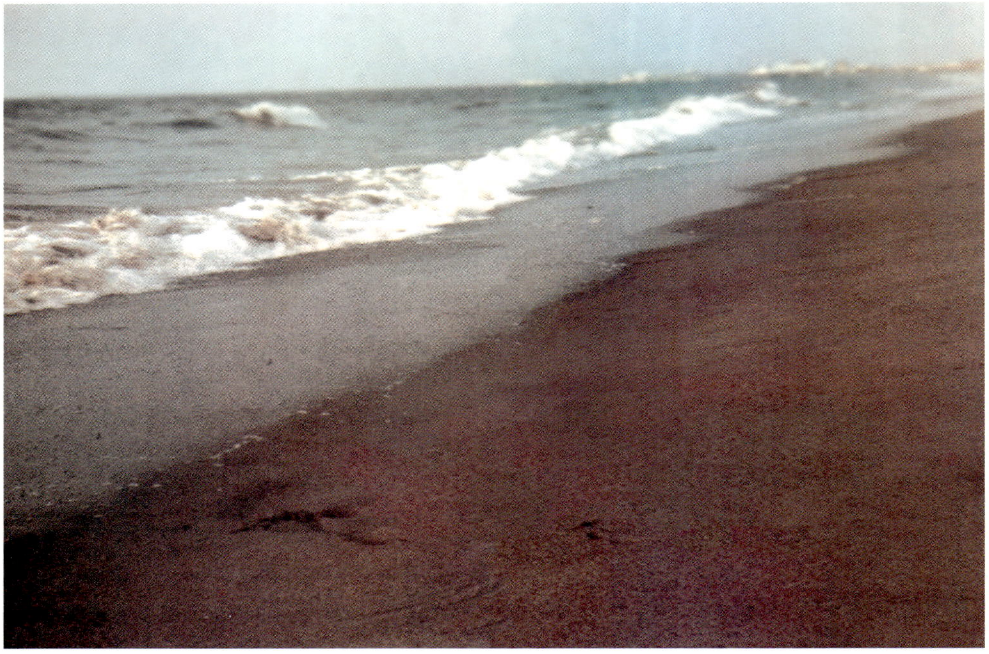

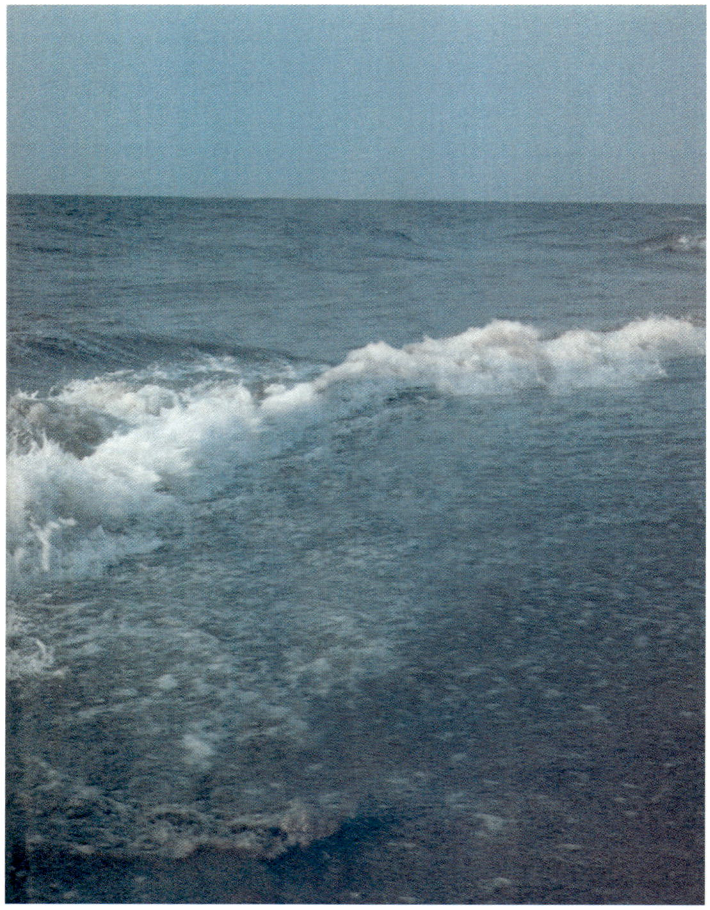

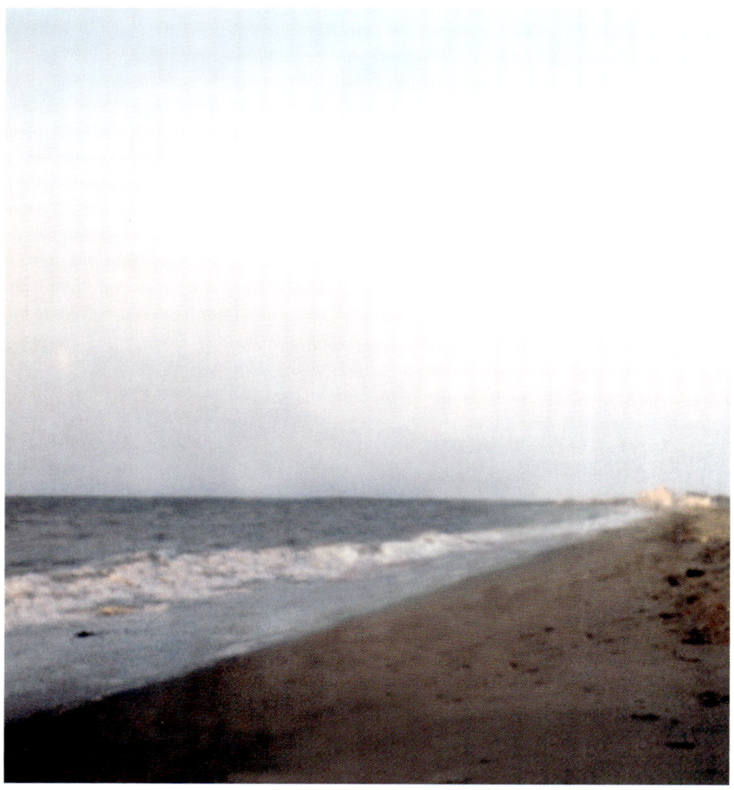

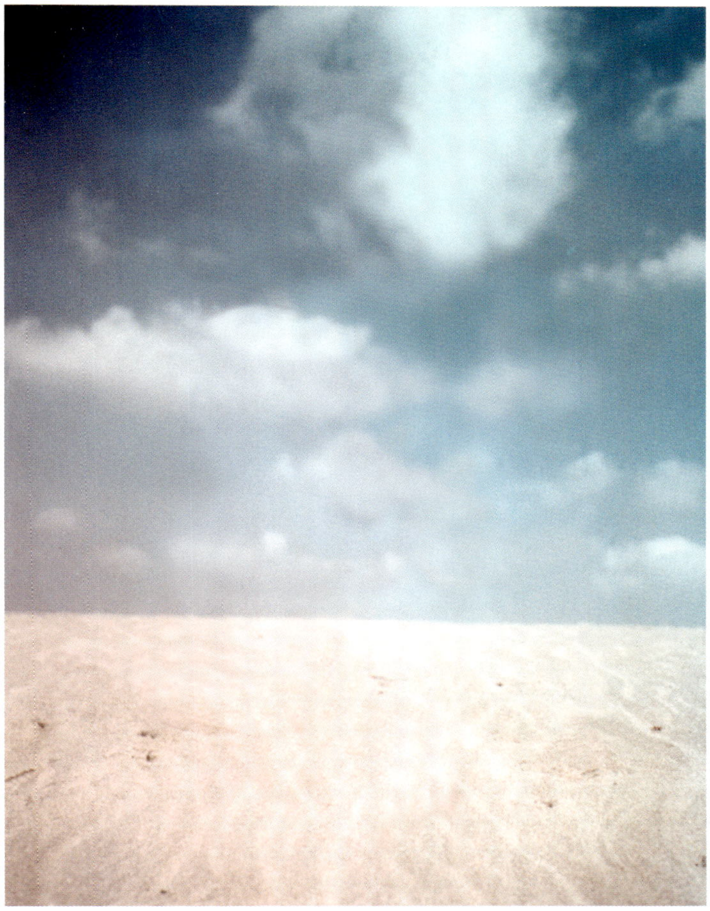
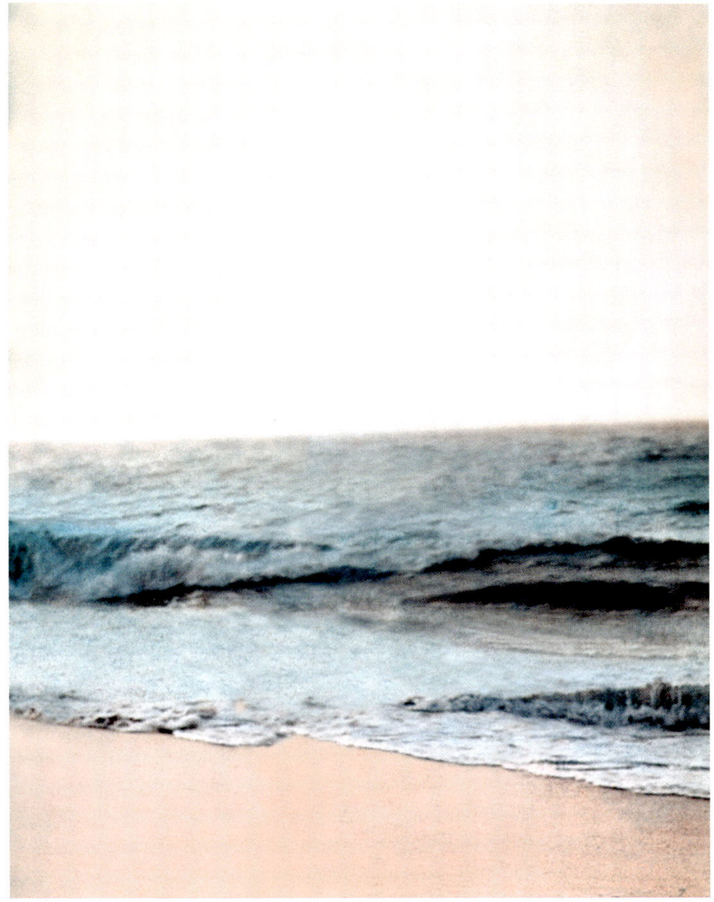
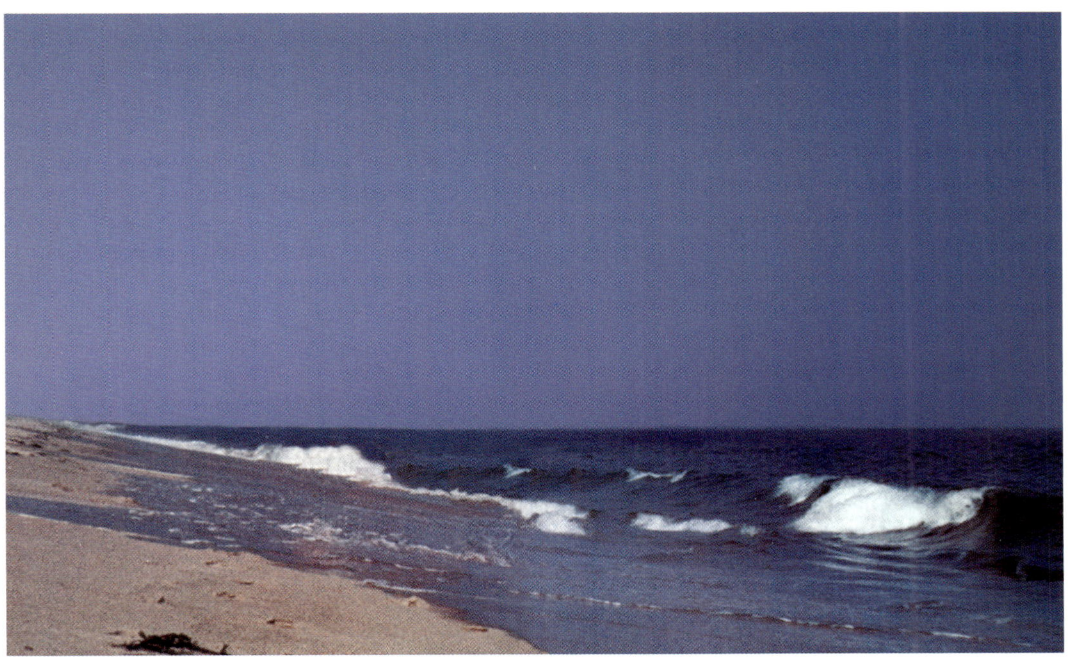

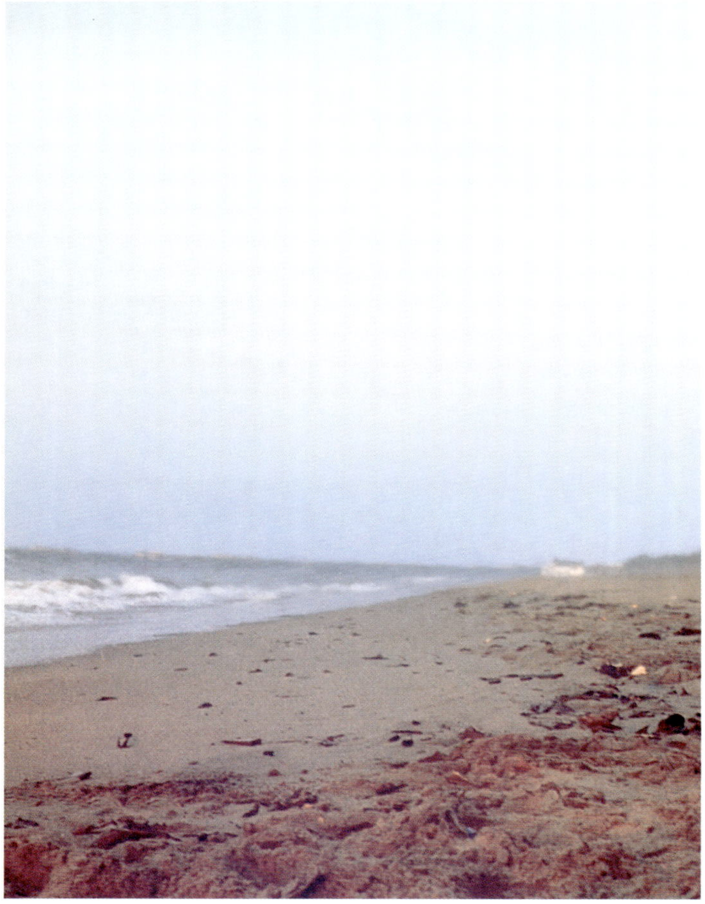

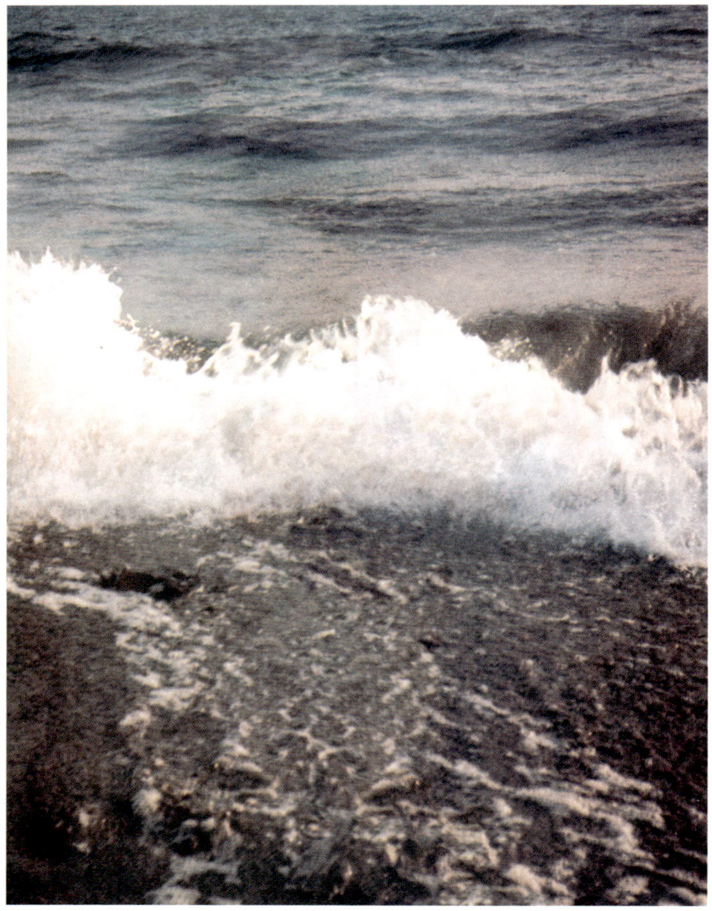

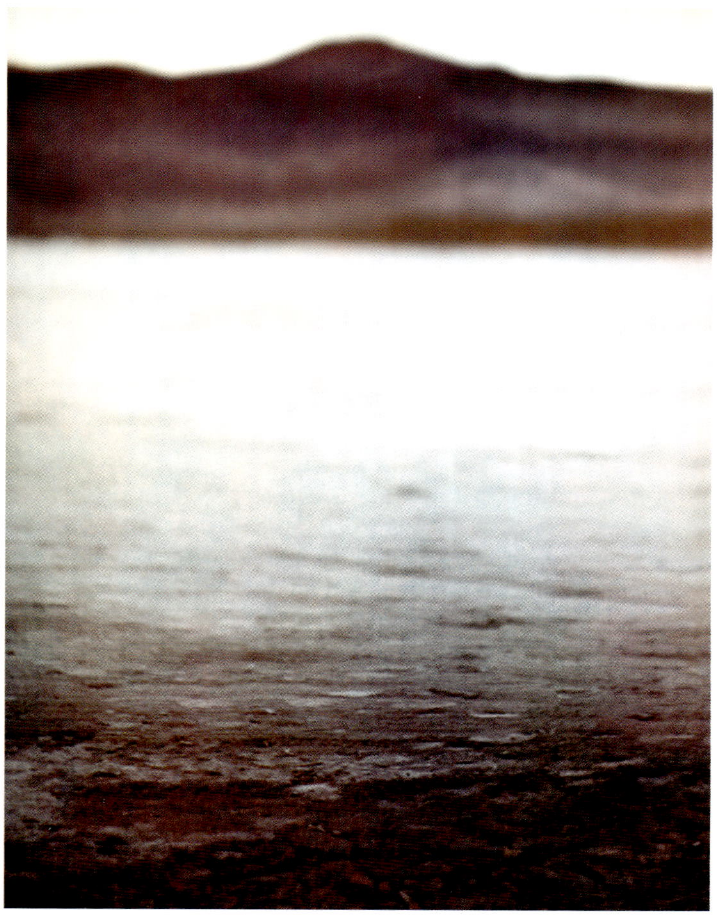

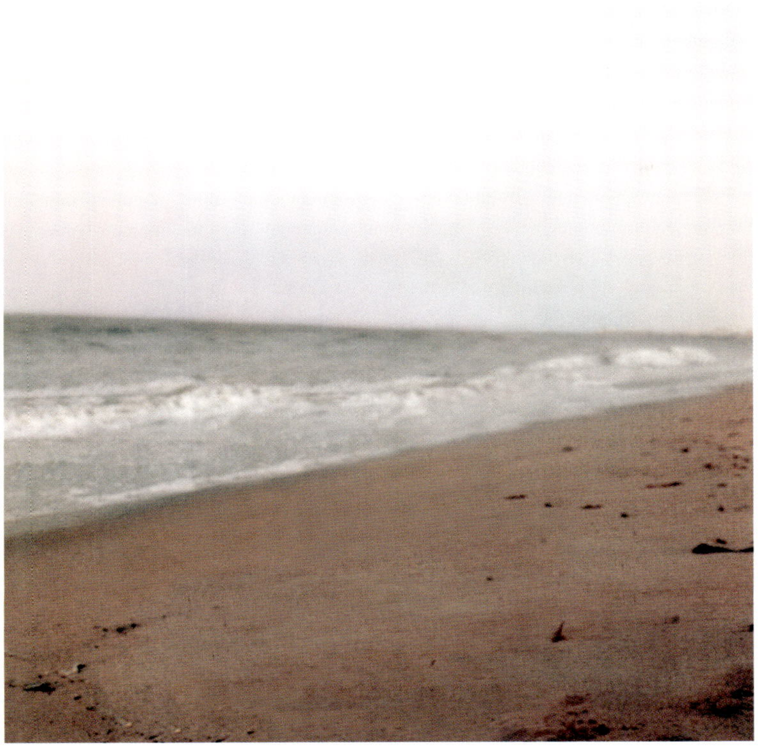

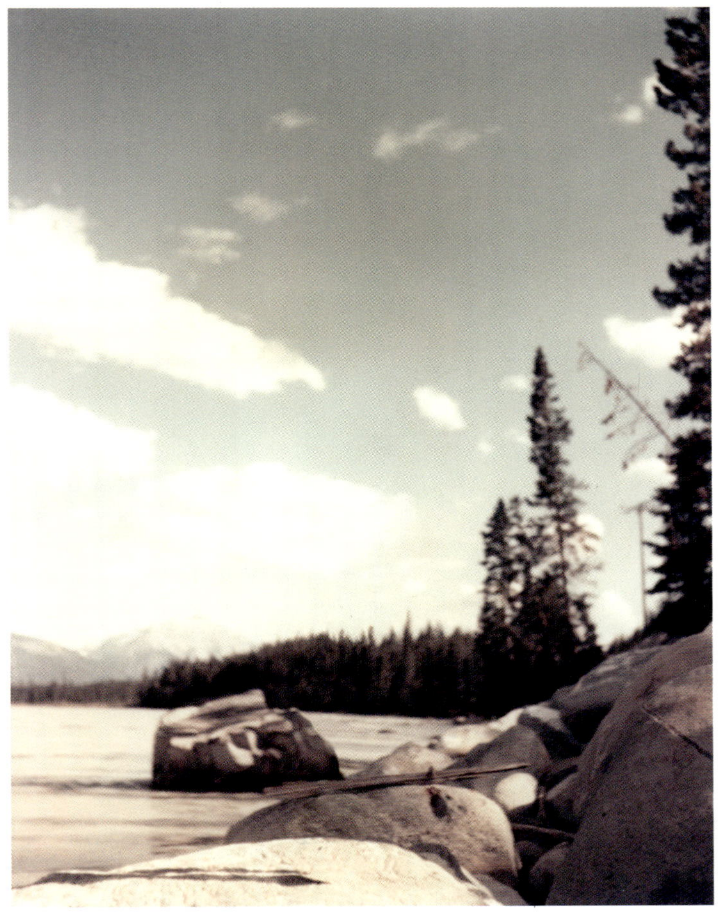

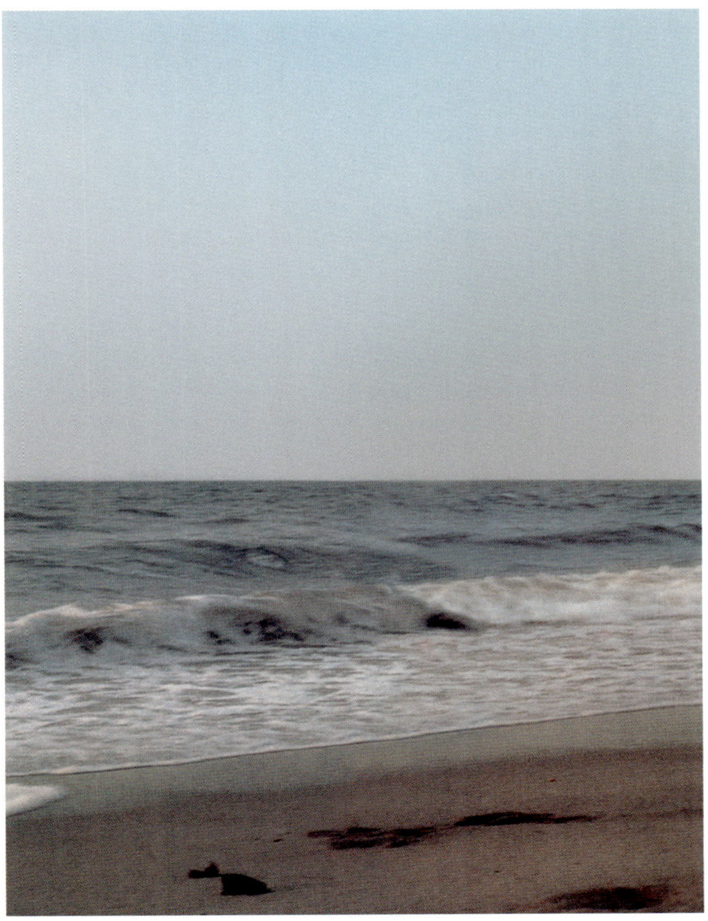

DANK

Wir danken allen Personen und Institutionen, die am Zustandekommen der Ausstellung und des Kataloges mitgewirkt haben. In erster Linie den Leihgebern für ihr Vertrauen und die Großzügigkeit, ihre Werke zu Verfügung zu stellen. Thomas Ruff für das wunderbare Gespräch mit Paul Pfeiffer und Stefano Basilico für das aufschlussreiche Essay sowie Lawrence Chua für sein ausgezeichnetes Lektorat dieser Texte. Nikolaus G. Schneider und Shaun Whiteside haben in bewährter Weise die Übersetzungen der Texte ins Deutsche und Englische besorgt, Anna Wesek hat dem Katalog eine äußerst attraktive Form gegeben. Christian Haye, Jenny Liu, Simon Preston und Jeffrey Uslip von The Project, New York und Los Angeles, Marie-Blanche Carlier und Ulrich Gebauer von carlier | gebauer in Berlin sowie Thomas Dane, Francois Chantala und Martine d'Anglejan-Chatillon von Thomas Dane, Inc. in London haben das Projekt mit vielfältigem Rat und Tat von Anfang an begleitet. Robin Vachel, Aaron Levi, John Letourneau, Onel Naar und Brigitte Landou, alle Mitarbeiter von Paul Pfeiffer, haben die Ausstellung verantwortungsvoll und mit großem Enthusiasmus betreut. Ihnen allen gilt unser besonderer Dank.
Paul Pfeiffer sei schließlich ganz herzlich gedankt, für die vielen erhellenden Gespräche, die permanente Auseinandersetzung und vor allem für die wundervolle Ausstellung

ACKNOWLEDGEMENTS

We would like to thank all of the people and institutions who have helped prepare the exhibition and the catalogue. First and foremost all the lenders for their trust, and for the generosity they have shown in making their works available. Thomas Ruff for his wonderful conversation with Paul Pfeiffer, Stefano Basilico for his revealing essay, and Lawrence Chua for his expert editing of these texts. Nikolaus G. Schneider and Shaun Whiteside have translated the texts into German and English in proven fashion; and Anna Wesek has given the catalogue an extremely attractive form. Christian Haye, Jenny Liu, Simon Preston, and Jeffrey Uslip of The Project, New York and Los Angeles; Marie-Blanche Carlier and Ulrich Gebauer of carlier | gebauer in Berlin; and Thomas Dane, Francois Chantala and Martine d'Anglejan-Chatillon of Thomas Dane, Inc., London have all provided great help and advice since the very beginning of the project. Robin Vachal, Aaron Levi, John Letourneau, Onel Naar, and Brigitte Landou from Paul Pfeiffer's studio have taken care of the exhibition with great enthusiasm. Special thanks to all of them.
And finally, our warmest thanks to Paul Pfeiffer for the many enlightening conversations, the constant debates and above all for the fantastic exhibition.

LEIHGEBER / LENDERS

carlier | gebauer, Berlin
Thomas Dane, London

14 PRÄSENZ DER ABSENZ / THE PRESENCE OF ABSENCE
VALERIA LIEBERMANN

22 PAUL PFEIFFER—DISTURBING VISION
STEFANO BASILICO

62 PAUL PFEIFFER UND THOMAS RUFF IM GESPRÄCH / PAUL PFEIFFER AND THOMAS RUFF IN CONVERSATION

4 24 LANDSCAPES
28 FOUR HORSEMEN OF THE APOCALYPSE
38 ORPHEUS DESCENDING
40 MORNING AFTER THE DELUGE
42 CARYATID
44 THREE STUDIES OF FIGURES AT THE BASE OF A CRUCIFIXION
50 THE LONG COUNT (RUMBLE IN THE JUNGLE)
52 THE LONG COUNT (I SHOOK UP THE WORLD)
54 THE LONG COUNT (THRILLA IN MANILA)
56 DUTCH INTERIOR
58 SELF-PORTRAIT AS A FOUNTAIN

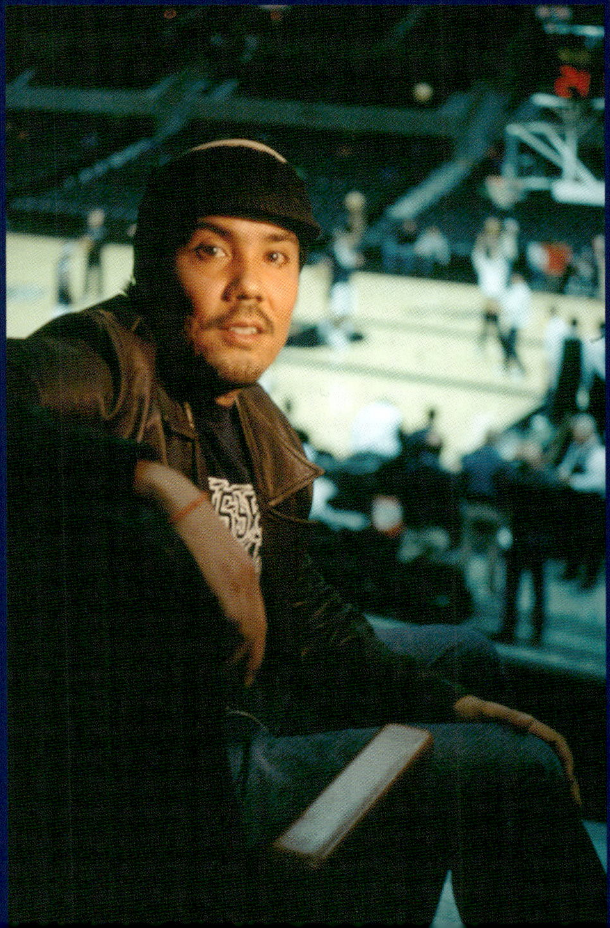

PRÄSENZ DER ABSENZ
THE PRESENCE OF ABSENCE

VALERIA LIEBERMANN

Bei jeder Bildbetrachtung ist es zu beobachten. Das Auge wandert immer wieder unmittelbar in den Mittelpunkt des Bildes, während die anderen Ebenen, wie beispielsweise der Mittel- und Hintergrund entweder an den Rand des Interesses geraten oder komplett ausgeblendet werden. Wie kann man jedoch das Auge davon abhalten ins Bildzentrum zu wandern? Oder es, entgegen seines normalen Perzeptionsvorgangs, dazu bewegen, sich auch mit der Peripherie zu beschäftigen?

Mit dieser Frage befasst sich Paul Pfeiffer seit mehreren Jahren und sucht nach Wegen, »to visually level the playing field, to keep the viewer's eye from wandering toward the center.«[1] Eines der Mittel, die Pfeiffer bei der Erstellung seiner Skulpturen, Videos und Fotografien einsetzt, um den Betrachter in das Bild zu holen und sein Interesse aus dem Bildzentrum zu ziehen, ist die Schaffung von mehr oder weniger offensichtlichen »Leerstellen«. Meist sind es die Akteure, die man im Zentrum des jeweiligen Bildes erwarten würde, die verschwunden, ausgelöscht oder in ihrer Bedeutung für das Bild negiert wurden. Und doch sind sie immer noch latent vorhanden, da Pfeiffer kollektive Medienbilder, wie Fotografien und Filmaufnahmen von Stars aus Film, Sport oder Showbusiness sowie berühmte Filmsequenzen als Vorlage oder Ausgangspunkt benutzt. Denn bei diesen Bildern kann er sicher sein, dass das Ausgangsbild im visuellen Speicher des Betrachters vorhanden ist und er dadurch die Fehlstelle spürt oder bewusst wahrnimmt.

Am deutlichsten wird dies bei *Self-Portrait as a Fountain,* das auf eine der einprägsamsten Filmszenen der Geschichte Hollywoods zurückgreift: auf die berühmte Duschsequenz aus Alfred Hitchcocks Film *Psycho*[2]. Für die Herstellung der Videoskulptur löste Pfeiffer das prägnanteste Detail des Filmes – die Dusche – aus seinem erzählerischen Zusammenhang und stellt es in 1,5-facher Vergrößerung in den Ausstellungsraum. Die scheinbare Filmkulisse wird durch technisches Filmgerät, wie Traversen und Scheinwerfer sowie neun in die Dusche hereinragende Überwachungskameras ergänzt. Mit Hilfe eines an die Seite gestellten Wassertanks läuft beständig Wasser aus dem großen Duschkopf, was dazu beiträgt die Szenerie noch realer wirken zu lassen. Auf einem kleinen Monitor, der auf dem Boden an der Rückseite der Dusche steht, sieht man die von den Überwachungskameras aufgefangenen Bilder, die an die verschiedenen, bekannten Filmbilder der Szene aus Psycho erinnern – allerdings ohne die für Hitchcock typische »Suspense«. Obgleich alles fehlt, was die Szene so unverwechselbar machte – die beteiligten Personen, der Regisseur, die Schauspieler und das Filmteam, oder die Requisiten, die Blut suggerierende Flüssigkeit im Abfluss und das Messer – erkennt man die Szene dennoch sofort. Die Akteure werden durch die

It's something you can experience every time you look at a picture. The eye repeatedly wanders to the centre of the picture, while the other levels, such as the middleground and the background, are either marginalised in terms of our interest, or completely faded out. But how can we keep the eye from wandering to the centre of the picture? Or help it, contrary to its normal perceptual process, to engage with the periphery as well?

Paul Pfeiffer has been preoccupied with this question for several years, seeking ways »to visually level the playing field, to keep the viewer's eye from wandering toward the center.«[1] One of the devices that he uses in making his sculptures, videos and photographs, to bring the viewer into the picture and draw his interest away from the center of the picture, is the creation of more or less obvious »absences«. In most cases it is the protagonist that one would expect to see at the centre of the picture, who has disappeared, been expunged or had its importance for the image negated. And yet they remain a latent presence, since Pfeiffer uses as his models or source material collective media images, such as photographs and stills of stars from film, sport or show-business, as well as famous film sequences. For in these pictures he can be sure that the source image is present in the viewer's visual storehouse, and that he will consequently sense its absence, or consciously perceive it.

This is most clearly apparent in *Self-Portrait as a Fountain,* which refers to one of the most memorable film scenes in Hollywood history: the famous shower sequence from Alfred Hitchcock's film *Psycho*[2]. To make the video sculpture, Pfeiffer freed the most succinct detail of the film – the shower – from its narrative context, and placed it in the exhibition space enlarged one and a half times. The apparent film-set is complemented by technical film equipment, such as cross-beams and spotlights, as well as nine surveillance cameras protruding into the shower. Water runs constantly out of the big shower-head from a water-tank placed at the side, and this helps to make the set appear even more real. A small monitor standing on the floor at the back of the shower shows the pictures recorded by the surveillance cameras, which recall the various familiar shots from the scene from *Psycho* – although without Hitchcock's trademark suspense. Although it lacks all the things that made the scene so unmistakeable – the people involved, the director, the actors and the film crew, or the props, the liquid suggesting blood in the plughole and the knife – we still recognise the scene immediately. The protagonists are replaced by the cameras, some of which precisely match Hitchcock's camera angles. The position of the director is taken by the viewer himself, and at that point he also replaces the absent props in his imagination. Just as Hitchcock always made a shadowy appearance for a moment in his films, so that one could never be quite sure that one had really

1. »Paul Pfeiffer and John Baldessari in Conversation«, in: *Paul Pfeiffer*, Ausst.-Kat. MIT Visual Arts Center, Cambridge and the Museum of Contemporary Art, Chicago, Chicago 2003, S. 33

2. *Psycho* ist nicht nur einer der berühmtesten Filme von Alfred Hitchcock, sondern auch einer der ungewöhnlichsten im Sinne von Technik und Darstellung. Hitchcock drehte den Film 1960 in Schwarzweiß und im Fernsehformat, anstatt wie bei seinen vorhergehenden Filmen in Farbe und im Kinoformat. Zusätzlich setzt Hitchcock hier das erste Mal die Mittel des Horrorfilms ein und kombiniert sexuelle Prägung mit brutalem Verbrechen. Die wichtigste Szene des Films, die Ermordung der von Janet Leigh dargestellten jungen Frau unter der Dusche, legt die tiefsten Ängste jedes Einzelnen bloß. Die größtmögliche Intimität, der nackte Körper unter der Dusche, wird durch den Mörder zerstört. Zusätzlich erlaubt sich Hitchcock in dem Film, die Identifikationsfigur für die Zuschauer bereits nach circa einer halben Stunde aus dem Film auszulöschen und nur noch als Erinnerungsspur beizubehalten.

1. »Paul Pfeiffer and John Baldessari in Conversation«, in: *Paul Pfeiffer*, exhibition catalogue MIT Visual Arts Center Cambridge and the Museum of Contemporary Art, Chicago, Chicago 2003, p. 33

2. *Psycho* is not just one of Alfred Hitchcock's most famous films, but also one of the most unusual in terms of technique and representation. Hitchcock made the film in 1960, in black and white and in television format, as opposed to his earlier films, which were made in colour and in cinema format. In addition, he uses the devices of the horror film for the first time, and links sexual subject-matter with violent crime. The most important scene in the film, the murder in the shower of the young woman played by Janet Leigh, lays bare the deepest fears of every individual.

anwesenden Kameras ersetzt, von denen einige exakt den Kameraeinstellungen Hitchcocks entsprechen. Die Position des Regisseurs wird vom Betrachter selbst eingenommen, der in dem Moment auch die fehlenden Requisiten in seiner Imagination ersetzt. So wie Hitchcock in seinen Filmen immer für einen Augenblick schattenartig erschien, so dass man sich nie sicher sein konnte, ihn wirklich gesehen zu haben, blitzt hier durch die Zusammenführung von »realer« Filmszenerie und kollektivem Filmbild die Erinnerung an die Szene im Kopf des Betrachters auf. Und doch stellt sich die Frage, ob man nicht noch mehr sieht, außer einer Dusche und suggestiven Filmbildern. Denn gerade das »Nichts«, die leere Dusche, lädt den Rezipienten ein, gleichzeitig Zuschauer und Akteur der Bildinszenierung zu werden, was ihn in den Mittelpunkt des Geschehens geraten lässt. Folgt der Betrachter der Bildstrategie, so findet er sich nicht nur in einer berühmten Filmszene wieder, sondern auch mitten in der Diskussion um die Auswirkungen der Massenmedien auf das Privatleben. Die technischen Entwicklungen im Medienbereich, sei es bei Fernsehübertragungen oder bei Webcams im Internet, erlauben immer mehr das Eindringen der Öffentlichkeit in das private Leben. Die Dusche, die als Symbol größter Intimität gesehen werden kann, wird durch die an Speere erinnernden Kameras in ihrer Integrität verletzt.

Konnte der Betrachter bei *Self-Portrait as a Fountain* zwischen den verschiedenen Positionen, der des Kameramanns beziehungsweise Regisseurs, des Schauspielers und auch des Zuschauers hin und herwechseln, so ist er bei *Dutch Interior* Beobachtender und Beobachteter in einer Person. Denn um hinter den Ursprung der lebensgroßen Projektion eines altertümlich wirkenden, menschenleeren Innenraumes zu kommen, muss er durch ein kleines, auf den ersten Blick nicht erkennbares Loch in der Projektionswand schauen. Von dort blickt er ins Innere eines Treppenhauses, das sich als puppenstubenartiges Modell zu erkennen gibt. Indem er sich der Projektionsfläche annähert, tritt er physisch in das Bild ein, das sich nun auf seinem Rücken als Projektion abzeichnet. Paradoxerweise wird er sich erst in dem Moment des Modells bewusst, in welchem eine, die Projektion aufnehmende Kamera versteckt ist, in dem er Teil des Bildes wird. Von seiner Neugier getrieben wird der Betrachter im gleichen Augenblick »Voyeur« und auch »Objekt der Betrachtung«. Die Blickrichtungen, die Pfeiffer vorgibt – sowohl die des Gucklochs als auch die der Kamera –, entsprechen den Kameraeinstellungen des in den 1970er Jahren gedrehten Horrorfilms *Amityville Horror*, von dem das Vorbild des Modells stammt. In diesem Film gibt sich das Böse, ähnlich wie bei vielen anderen Horrorfilmen, nicht zu erkennen, sondern ist immer das unsichtbare Auge, das die Protagonisten verfolgt. Das Unbehagen, das durch die Leere und Bewegungslosigkeit des Bildes im Betrachter aufsteigt

seen him, the memory of the scene flashes through the viewer's mind as he brings together the »real« film set and the collective film image. And yet one wonders whether one doesn't see something else, beyond a shower and suggestive film images. Because it is precisely the »absence«, the empty shower, that invites the recipient to be at once an onlooker and a protagonist in the staging of the image, and thus to enter the centre of events. If the viewer follows the pictorial strategy, he finds himself not only inside a famous film scene, but also in the middle of a discussion of the effects of the mass media on private life. Technical developments within the media, whether in television broadcasts or internet webcams, allow an even greater penetration of the public sphere into private life. The shower, which can be seen as a symbol of a high level of intimacy, has its integrity violated by the spear-like cameras.

If, in *Self-Portrait as a Fountain*, the viewer was able to switch back and forth between the various positions, that of the cameraman or director, of the actor and also of the viewer, in Dutch Interior he is at once observer and observed. Because in order to get behind the source of the life-sized projection of an old-fashioned-looking, deserted inner space, he must look through a small hole in the projection wall, which cannot at first be seen. From that vantage point he looks into a staircase, which looks like a doll's-house model. As he approaches the screen, he physically enters the picture, which now appears as a projection on his back. Paradoxically, he becomes aware of the model, which contains a camera recording the projection, only at the moment when he becomes part of the picture. Driven by his curiosity, the viewer becomes at once a »voyeur« and a »viewed object«. The lines of vision set by Pfeiffer – both that of the peephole and that of the camera – correspond to the camera angles of the seventies' horror film *Amityville Horror*, which is the source of the model. In that film, as in many other horror films, evil is not visible, but is always the invisible eye following the protagonists. The mounting unease provoked in the viewer by the emptiness and motionlessness, and intensified by his »voyeuristic act«, thus has two sources: the viewer's publicly displayed curiosity and his intuitive insight into the picture source. But the effect of the irritation of perception is even more intense in that the viewer is forced to acknowledge that the levels of reality have shifted. The life-sized projected image emanates from a doll's house sized model, which in turn copies a real, life-sized film set. The projected reality is not real, but rather the reality of a media image.

In *Morning after the Deluge*, Pfeiffer once again symbolically inverts our seeing habits and blurs the bounds of perception. Over a long period of time he filmed sunrises and sunsets in Cape Cod, before digitally editing them together into a twenty-minutes film[3]. In this work the sun, contrary to visible reality, remains motionless at the

The greatest possible intimacy, the naked body under the shower, is destroyed by the murderer. In addition, Hitchcock allows himself to erase from the film, after almost half an hour, the main character with whom the viewers will have identified, and to keep her in the film only as a trace in memory.

und durch seine »voyeuristische Tat« unter Umständen verstärkt wird, rührt daher von zwei Quellen: von der öffentlich zur Schau gestellten Neugier und dem unbewussten Erspüren der Bildquelle. Noch stärker wirkt sich allerdings die Irritation der Wahrnehmung aus, da der Betrachter erkennen muss, dass sich die Realitätsebenen verschoben haben. Das lebensgroß projizierte Bild stammt von einem puppenstubenartigen Modell, das wiederum eine reale, lebensgroße Filmkulisse nachahmt. Die projizierte Realität ist nicht real, sondern die in zwei Schritten übertragene Realität eines medialen Bildes.

Mit *Morning after the Deluge* stellt Pfeiffer erneut unsere Sehgewohnheiten sinnbildlich auf den Kopf und verwischt Wahrnehmungsgrenzen. Über einen längeren Zeitraum hatte er in Cape Cod Sonnenaufgänge und -untergänge gefilmt, die er anschließend digital zu einem zwanzigminütigen Film zusammen fügte[3]. In dieser Arbeit bleibt nun die Sonne, entgegen der sichtbaren Realität, unbeweglich in der Mitte der Projektion stehen, während der Horizont und winzige Details wie Vögel oder Flugzeuge sich durch das statische Bild der Sonne bewegen. Dies entspricht zwar der naturwissenschaftlichen Regel, dass sich die Erde und nicht die Sonne bewegt, aber nicht dem, was man sieht. »The viewer is torn between two contradictory realities coexisting on a single picture plane. There is the reality of the sun rising and setting behind the earth's horizon and the opposing reality of the earth's horizon moving across the surface of the sun. The resulting split sense of reality in the eye of the beholder is the real theme and subject of *Morning after the Deluge*.«[4] Nur noch das Bild der Sonne und die Weite des Himmels und des Wassers bestimmen das Bild, dessen Titel *Der Morgen nach der Sintflut* auf das Ende und den möglichen Neuanfang des Lebens anspielt – ein Naturereignis par excellence. Und doch war es erst der Computer und die damit verbundenen Programme, die es Pfeiffer ermöglichten eine perfekte Simulation der Welt herzustellen und alles Menschliche verschwinden zu lassen. Vom Naturschauspiel bleibt nur die Leere der mechanischen Reproduktion und die suggestive Sprache des wiederholbaren Bildes. Der Betrachter hingegen ist außen vor. Er schwankt nicht nur zwischen den Realitätsebenen, sondern auch zwischen rationaler Wahrnehmung und emotionaler Sinnesempfindung.

Neben der Frage nach dem Beobachter und dem Beobachtetem im Prozess der Wahrnehmung steht für Pfeiffer die Frage nach Identität, ihrer Entstehung und ihrer Rekonstruktion in einer von den Massenmedien bestimmten Welt. Dabei interessieren den Künstler vor allem die von den Medien verbreiteten Bilder von Stars, die tief in das kollektive Bewusstsein jedes Einzelnen innerhalb der globalen Gesellschaft eingedrungen sind. Mit Hilfe dieser Bilder kann er die konstruierte Identität der Stars bewusst machen, welche die eigentliche Persönlichkeit

3. Die Aufnahmen des Sonnenuntergangs wurden auf den Kopf gestellt und so in die Aufnahmen des Sonnenaufgangs eingebaut, dass die Sonne immer als volle Scheibe zu sehen ist.

4. Aussage des Künstlers, zitiert nach: Jane Farver, »Morning after the Deluge«, in: *Paul Pfeiffer*, Ausst.Kat. MIT Visual Arts Center, Cambridge and the Museum of Contemporary Art, Chicago, Chicago 2003, S. 46

centre of the projection, while the horizon and tiny details like birds or aeroplanes cross the static image of the sun. This may correspond to the scientific rule that it is the earth and not the sun that moves, but it does not correspond to what one sees. »The viewer is torn between two contradictory realities coexisting on a single picture plane. There is the reality of the sun rising and setting behind the earth's horizon and the opposing reality of the earth's horizon moving across the surface of the sun. The resulting split sense of reality in the eye of the beholder is the real theme and subject of *Morning after the Deluge*.«[4]

The picture of the sun and the expanse of sky and water are all that define the image, whose title refers to the end and the possible new beginning of life – a natural event *par excellence*. And yet it is only computers and their programmes that allowed Pfeiffer to produce a perfect simulation of the world and cause everything human to disappear. All that remains of the natural spectacle is the emptiness of mechanical reproduction and the suggestive language of the repeatable image. The viewer, on the other hand, stands outside. He not only oscillates between levels of reality, but also between rational perception and emotional sensation.

For Pfeiffer, alongside the question of the observer and the observed in the process of perception there stands the question of identity, its origin and its reconstruction in a world defined by the mass media. What interests the artist most is the pictures of stars distributed by the media, which have penetrated deep into the collective consciousness of every individual within global society. Using these pictures, he is able to create an awareness of the constructed identity of the stars that makes the actual personality disappear behind a media façade. At the same time he shows how the individual takes his bearings from these artificially constructed role models of media society. The unconscious relationships between the individual and the object of his desire and admiration play a large part in this. Icons from the worlds of film and sport, such as Marilyn Monroe or Muhammad Ali, are particularly well suited to lay bare the creation of the star cult, constructed appearance and global fandom. Rather than yet again placing the stars at the centre of events, Pfeiffer digitally erases the »object of interest«, or rather overlays the picture of the star with the surrounding background – and in this way he in a sense reverses the relationship of figure and ground, by making the background the most important thing in the picture and creating space for the viewer's trail-hunting.

In the three versions of *The Long Count* he uses television shots of the last rounds of three important boxing matches by Cassius Clay, alias Muhammad Ali, for his three-minute loops. These are the fights against Sonny Liston in Miami Beach, 1964 (*I Shook Up The World*), against George Foreman in Kinshasa, 1974 (*Rumble in the Jungle*) and against Joe Frazier in Manila, 1975 (*Thrilla in Manila*). His films do not

3. The shots of sunset have been inverted and incorporated into the shots of sunrise in such a way that the sun always appears as a complete disc.

4. Statement by the artist, quoted in: Jane Farver, »Morning after the Deluge«, in: *Paul Pfeiffer*, exhibition catalogue MIT Visual Arts Center, Cambridge, and the Museum of Contemporary Art, Chicago, Chicago 2003, p. 46

hinter einer mediengerechten Fassade verschwinden lässt. Gleichzeitig zeigt er die Orientierung des Individuums an diesen künstlich geschaffenen Rollenmodellen der Mediengesellschaft. Gerade die unbewussten Beziehungen zwischen dem Einzelnen und dem Objekt seiner Begierde und Bewunderung spielen eine große Rolle. Film- und Sportikonen, wie Marilyn Monroe oder Muhammad Ali eignen sich besonders, um die Schaffung von Starkult, konstruierter Erscheinung und globaler Begeisterung offen zu legen. Anstatt die Stars erneut ins Zentrum des Geschehens zu holen, löscht Pfeiffer das »Objekt des Interesses« digital aus, oder besser, er überdeckt das Bild des Stars mit dem umgebenden Hintergrund – und kehrt so in gewisser Weise das Verhältnis von Figur und Grund um, indem der Hintergrund die Hauptsache des Bildes wird und Platz für die Spurensuche des Betrachters schafft. Bei den drei Versionen von *The Long Count* benutzt er Fernsehaufnahmen der jeweils letzten Runde von drei wichtigen Boxkämpfen von Cassius Clay alias Muhammad Ali für die dreiminütigen Loops. Es handelt sich dabei um die Kämpfe gegen Sonny Liston, 1964 in Miami Beach (*I Shook Up The World*), gegen George Foreman, 1974 in Kinshasa (*Rumble in the Jungle*) und gegen Joe Frazier, 1975 in Manila (*Thrilla in Manila*). Seine Filme zeigen jedoch nicht die Dramatik des Kampfes, sondern führen sie als geisterhafte Schattenspiele vor. Die Boxer und die Kampfrichter sind nur noch als sich bewegende, durchsichtige Formen zu erahnen, während der sie umgebende Raum, der Boxring und die Zuschauer in den Mittelpunkt des Interesses treten. Nicht die Boxer oder der Boxkampf, sondern die Zuschauer, die den Kampf verfolgen, werden zum Inhalt des Bildes. Denn sie sind die einzigen, die etwas »sehen«, die auf das Geschehen im Ring reagieren und es kommentieren. Der Betrachter vor dem Monitor nimmt daher nicht mehr den eigentlichen Boxkampf, sondern den durch die Reaktionen der Zuschauer übertragenen Kampf – und somit eine gefilterte Sicht wahr, an der er das »Sehen« und »Beobachten« ablesen kann. Von der ursprünglichen Handlung des Spektakels bleibt nur eine leere, gespensterhafte Fläche zurück. Pfeiffer nimmt mit seiner Bearbeitung dem Spektakel die Macht, die Grenzen der Imagination festzulegen und gibt dem Betrachter die Möglichkeit, die Zusammenhänge selbst herausfiltern und bestimmen zu können.

Bei der Bearbeitung der drei Versionen von *The Long Count* ist es dem Künstler wichtig, dass man die Boxer und die Ringrichter noch schattenhaft wahrnimmt, auch nachdem sie entfernt wurden. Denn dadurch ergibt sich eine dauerhafte Spur, die zwar nicht mehr die Akteure zeigt, aber durch die Störung der Oberfläche des Bildes das Geschehen anders lesbar werden lässt. Die Störung scheint auf die Hintergründe und Ursprünge der Entstehung von ikonischen Bildern in Amerika zu verweisen. Es sind die medialen Spektakel, die großen, vom Fern-

show the drama of the fight, however, instead presenting it as a ghostly shadow-play. The boxers and the referee can be sensed only as moving, transparent forms, while the surrounding space, the boxing ring and the spectators, become the centre of interest. The content of the picture is no longer the boxers or the boxing match, but the spectators following the match. Because they are the only ones who can »see« something, and who react to events in the ring and comment upon it. Consequently the viewer in front of the monitor no longer perceives the actual boxing match, but the match conveyed by the spectators' reactions – and thus a filtered vision, from which he can read »seeing« and »observing«. All that remains of the original content of the spectacle is an empty, ghostly surface. Through his treatment of it, Pfeiffer robs the spectacle of its power to establish the boundaries of the imagination, and gives the viewer the opportunity to filter out and determine the connections himself.

In the treatment of the three versions of *The Long Count,* the artist considers it important that we still have a shadowy perception of the boxers and referees even after they have been removed. For a lasting trace remains which, although it no longer shows the protagonists, allows us to read events in a different way through the disturbance of the surface of the picture. The disturbance seems to refer to the backgrounds and sources of the origin of iconic images in America. It is the media spectacles, the major sport and music events broadcast live on television, the Hollywood films and the related star careers that are manifested in these iconic images, and have an immediate effect on the individual. On the one hand these pictures make a significant contribution to the alteration and extinction of historical consciousness, since what is important in them is not the star as a person or the place as a real historical place, but the star as prototype and the artificially created, often timeless atmosphere as a reference point. On the other hand they do effect a change in the consciousness of the individual, which only now appears to exist for the viewing public. In the media age, the viewer's perspective becomes the most important factor in self-perception and the finding of identity.

Marilyn Monroe seems to have been one such almost prototypical person, who seemed only to exist for and through the external gaze. In the *24 Landscapes* Pfeiffer turned, amongst other things, to various photographs that George Barris took of Marilyn Monroe on a beach in California in June and July 1962. He has combined them with other photographs of Monroe by the sea or a lake, and in all of them – unlike Ali's boxing matches – he has completely erased the image of the star from the picture, without leaving a single trace. He thus guides the eye to deserted, romantic-looking landscape photographs that create a strange feeling of loneliness, peace and emptiness. For Pfeiffer, it was not the picture of the star that occupied the foreground,

sehen live übertragenen Sport- oder Musik-Events, die in Hollywood entstehenden Filme und die damit verbundenen Starkarrieren, die sich in diesen ikonischen Bildern manifestieren und eine unmittelbare Wirkung auf das Individuum besitzen. Einerseits tragen diese Bilder wesentlich zur Veränderung und Auslöschung von historischem Bewusstsein bei, da nicht der Star als Person oder der Ort als realer historischer Ort wichtig ist, sondern der Star als Prototyp und das künstlich geschaffene, oft zeitlose Ambiente als Orientierungspunkt. Andererseits bewirken sie eine Veränderung im Bewusstsein des Individuums, das nun scheinbar erst für ein beobachtendes Publikum zu existieren beginnt. Die Beobachterperspektive wird im medialen Zeitalter zum wichtigsten Faktor der Selbst-Wahrnehmung und Identitätsfindung.
Marilyn Monroe scheint eine solche fast prototypische Person gewesen zu sein, die nur noch für und durch den Blick von Außen zu existieren schien. Daher verwundert es nicht, dass Pfeiffer Bilder Monroes für mehrere seiner Arbeiten benutzte. Bei den *24 Landscapes* griff er unter anderem auf verschiedene Fotografien von George Barris zurück, die dieser im Juni und Juli 1962 von Marilyn Monroe an einem Strand in Kalifornien aufnahm. Pfeiffer kombinierte sie mit anderen Fotografien Monroes am Meer oder einem See und löschte bei allen – im Unterschied zu den Boxkämpfen Alis – das Bild des Stars komplett, ohne jegliche Spur von ihr übrig zu lassen, aus dem Bild. Er lenkt dadurch den Blick auf menschenleere, romantisch anmutende Landschaftsaufnahmen, die ein seltsames Gefühl von Einsamkeit, Ruhe und Leere hinterlassen. Für Pfeiffer stand bei dieser Arbeit nicht das Bild des Stars im Vordergrund, sondern die Frage nach der Gültigkeit eines Bildes, dessen Existenzberechtigung genommen wurde. Mit Recht verweist Pfeiffer darauf, dass es Sinn macht, darüber nachzudenken, ob ein Bild auch ohne den Grund der Aufnahme noch gültig ist. Ist nicht schon der Hintergrund, die das eigentliche Bildthema umgebende Kulisse wichtig und als Bild interessant?
Pfeiffer gelingt es, eine neue, andere Art von Präsenz zu schaffen, indem er bei der Herstellung seiner Werke bewusst auf die Illusion eines bedeutsamen Bildes verzichtet. Es ist eine Präsenz der Abwesenheit – der Abwesenheit des Künstlers, des Akteurs und des offensichtlichen Bildthemas, oder umgekehrt eine Präsenz des Unsichtbaren. Er hebt die Bedeutung der als nebensächlich geltenden Faktoren eines Bildes hervor: den scheinbar unwichtigen Bildhintergrund und die Anwesenheit des Betrachters im und vor dem Bild. Dabei versucht er die verschiedenartigen Formen des Austauschs zwischen Betrachter und Werk in der heutigen, von einer Bilderflut geprägt Zeit auszuloten. Er scheint die These zu bestätigen, »..dass jeder Betrachter bereits eine Bibliothek visueller Erfahrungen,

but the question of the validity of an image once the justification for its existence had been removed. Pfeiffer rightly suggests that it makes sense to think about whether a picture retains its validity even without the reason for its being taken. Is the background, the backdrop for the actual theme of the picture, not itself important and interesting as a picture?
In the making of his works, Pfeiffer manages to create a new and different kind of presence while deliberately avoiding the illusion of a significant picture. A presence of absence – the absence of the artist, the person involved in the image and the obvious theme of the picture, as well as the presence of that which is inconspicious. He stresses the importance of the elements of an image that are usually considered secondary: the apparently unimportant background and the presence of the viewer in and in front of the picture. At the same time he tries to sound out the various forms of exchange between viewer and work in our own times, an age flooded by images. He seemed to confirm the theory »...that every viewer already stores in his head a library of visual experiences, fed by the mass media, from the movies to advertising posters«[5], and in this way connects the method of erasure with the strategy of the appropriation of found images. »What pushes me to use certain found images is that they have left a deep impression on me, either a long time ago, or very recently. The way images become burned into the memory shows how porous an individual identity really is.«[6] A great flood of pictures from a great variety of sources enters each individual's image-store, and become closely linked with his identity. For the artist, this in turn becomes inseparably connected with the making of art, and for the viewer with the act of viewing. Because one's own identity – however it may have been constructed – constantly pushes its way into the dialogue between the work and the artist, as well as that between the work and the viewer. In his work, the artist is unable to let his own identity and the inner pictures connected with it disappear, even though he may attempt to negate his personal signature. In looking at pictures, the viewer constantly seeks confirmation of his own ideas, his knowledge and thus of his identity. The pictures with which artist and viewer engage are thus not new, unknown pictures. Because in the media world there are no longer any images that are not located within a system of reference, which are not linked in one form or another with the identity of either the producer of the picture or the viewer. But the many absences that Pfeiffer incorporates into his works make the pictures look as though one had never seen them before. They help the eye to come out of the centre of the picture, and perceive the picture in its perfect entirety.

translated from German by Shaun Whiteside

5. Peter Weibel, »Das allusive Auge. Illusion, Anti-Illusion, Allusion«, in: *Fast Forward. Media Art Sammlung Goetz*, exhibition catalogue Zentrum für Kunst und Medientechnologie, Karlsruhe 2003, pp. 10-11

6. Paul Pfeiffer and John Baldessari in Conversation, in: *Paul Pfeiffer*, exhibition catalogue MIT Visual Arts Center, Cambridge and Museum of Contemporary Art, Chicago, Chicago 2003, pp. 36-37

gespeist aus den Massenmedien von Film bis zu Werbeplakaten, in seinem Kopf speichert«[5] und verbindet dergestalt die Methode der Auslöschung mit der Strategie der Aneignung von gefundenem Bildmaterial. »What pushes me to use certain found images is that they have left a deep impression on me, either a long time ago, or very recently. The way images become burned into the memory shows how porous an individual identity really is.«[6] Eine große Flut von Bildern, die aus verschiedensten Quellen stammen, dringen in den Bilderspeicher jedes einzelnen ein und verknüpfen sich eng mit dessen Identität. Diese wiederum verbindet sich für den Künstler untrennbar mit der Herstellung von Kunst und für den Betrachter mit der Betrachtung derselben. Denn die eigene Identität – wie auch immer sie sich konstruiert hat – schiebt sich permanent in den Dialog zwischen dem Werk und dem Künstler sowie dem Werk und dem Betrachter. Der Künstler kann in seiner Arbeit die eigene Identität und die damit verbundenen inneren Bilder nicht verschwinden lassen, auch wenn er die Negierung der persönlichen Handschrift anstrebt. Der Betrachter sucht bei der Betrachtung von Bildern stetig nach einer Bestätigung seiner eigenen Vorstellungen, seines Wissens und damit seiner Identität. Die Bilder mit denen sich Künstler und Betrachter beschäftigen, sind daher keine neuen, unbekannten Bilder. Denn in der medialen Welt gibt es keine Bilder mehr, die nicht verortet sind und nicht in der einen oder anderen Form mit der Identität des Bildproduzenten oder des Betrachters verknüpft sind. Die vielzähligen Leerstellen, die Pfeiffer in seine Werke einbaut, lassen die Bilder jedoch so erscheinen, als hätte man sie noch nie gesehen. Sie helfen dem Auge, aus dem Zentrum des Bildes herauszukommen und das Bild in seiner Vollkommenheit wahrzunehmen.

5. Peter Weibel, »Das allusive Auge. Illusion, Anti-Illusion, Allusion«, in: *Fast Forward. Media Art Sammlung Goetz*, Ausst.Kat. Zentrum für Kunst und Medientechnologie Karlsruhe 2003, S. 10-11

6. »Paul Pfeiffer and John Baldessari in Conversation«, in: *Paul Pfeiffer*, Ausst.kat. MIT List Visual Center, Cambridge and Museum of Contemporary Art, Chicago, Chicago 2003, S. 36/37

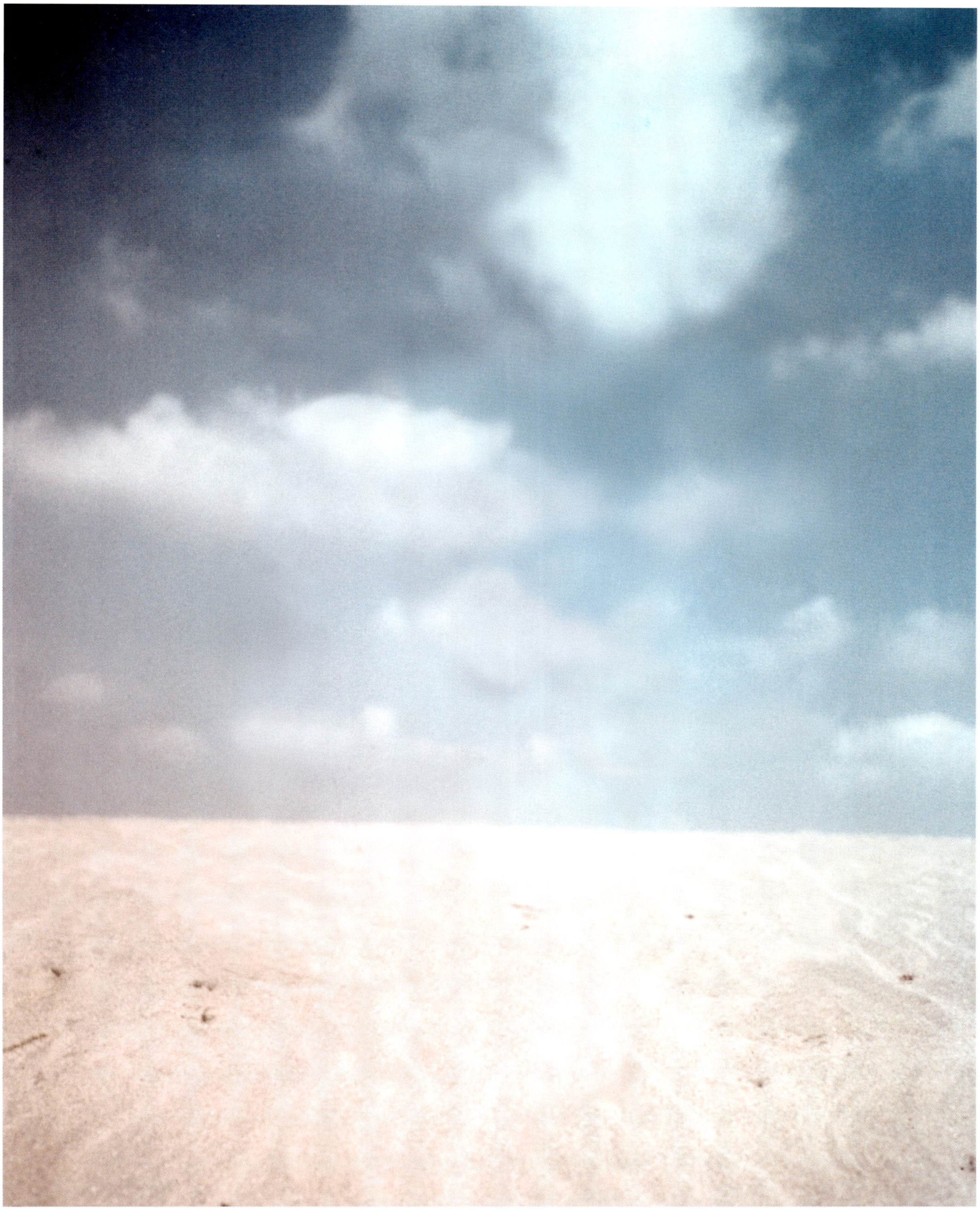

PAUL PFEIFFER
DISTURBING VISION

STEFANO BASILICO

Der Ring ist leer, und dennoch ist das Publikum gebannt. Dort, wo sich zwei Boxer befinden sollten, ist nichts als Luft und Schimmern und Wegducken und Zuschlagen. Die Seile biegen sich unter der Last eines Schwergewichtlers, der auf der Stelle festgenagelt und mit den Fäusten bearbeitet wird. Während das ursprüngliche Publikum dieses Sportereignisses jede kurze Gerade und jede Finte verfolgen kann, sind wir, die aktuellen Zuschauer, blind. Die Tatsache, dass in Pfeiffers Video *The Long Count (Thrilla in Manila)* der Hintergrund voll, der Vordergrund hingegen leer ist, deutet darauf hin, dass es in diesen Werken möglicherweise gar nicht um die Boxer, ja nicht einmal um ihre Entfernung geht, sondern vielmehr um das Publikum. In dieser Inszenierung einer unerwarteten Begegnung konfrontiert *The Long Count* zwei Arten von Publikum miteinander, nämlich Menschen, die sich den Boxkampf, und Menschen, die sich das Video ansehen. Dieser Vergleich ermöglicht es uns, einige Fragen zur Natur des Publikums und zu der des Zuschauerseins zu stellen. Ist ein Publikum mit dem anderen identisch? Verändert die Größe des Publikums – die Frage, ob es aus einer Person oder aus mehreren besteht – seinen Charakter? Führt das Sehen zu Einsichten oder steht es diesen eher im Weg? Die Beschäftigung mit einigen Werken Pfeiffers wird zeigen, dass der Künstler das Thema des Sehens und, wichtiger noch, das des Publikums immer wieder aufgegriffen hat.

»Immer den Ball im Auge behalten!« – diesen Ratschlag geben im Sport alle Trainer ihren Spielern, egal ob beim Football, beim Baseball oder beim Basketball. In der Videoarbeit *John 3:16* befindet sich die orangefarbene, leuchtende Kugel des Basketballs ständig in Bewegung, doch da sie in den Mittelpunkt gerückt wurde, statt herumwandern zu dürfen, sind wir im Stande, sie im Auge zu behalten, obwohl sie hin und her schwankt und sich dabei ständig um die eigene Achse dreht. Für diese Arbeit wählte Pfeiffer dutzende Videoclips von im Fernsehen übertragenen Basketballspielen aus, fügte diese unverbundenen Augenblicke dann zusammen und bearbeitete den Basketball selbst mit Hilfe des Motion-Track-Verfahrens, so dass der Ball auf der Stelle zu verharren scheint, während sich alles Übrige bewegt.[1] Im Gegensatz dazu, wie man ein Basketballspiel normalerweise erlebt, schränkt Pfeiffers Arbeit den Spielraum des Balles ein, indem sie ihm zwar ermöglicht, sich zu drehen, aber nicht, sich durch den Raum zu bewegen. Aufgrund dieses kleinen Eingriffs verändert sich das Verhältnis zwischen Gegenstand und Betrachter. Die traditionelle Struktur des Spiels wird umgekehrt. Der Ball scheint die Spieler und, als Folge hieraus, auch die Betrachter zu kontrollieren. Die Spieler schwärmen um den Ball herum, versuchen ihn zu ergreifen und zu werfen, aber er bewegt sich nicht, und sie verschwinden rasch aus dem Kamerabild. So wie Kopernikus die Tatsache, dass wir

1. Motion-tracking ist ein digitales Bearbeitungsverfahren, das es der Kamera ermöglicht, sich auf ein Detail des Bildes zu konzentrieren und anhand dieses Details die anderen im Videobild enthaltenen Informationen zu organisieren. Dieselbe Technik kommt später bei der Arbeit *Morning after the Deluge* zum Einsatz.

The ring is empty, but the audience is transfixed. Where there should be two boxers, there is only air, shimmering, and ducking, and jabbing. The ropes deflect with the weight of a heavyweight being pinned and pummeled. While the original audience of the event can follow every jab and every feint, we, the current audience, are blind. In Pfeiffer's video *The Long Count (Thrilla in Manila)*, the background is full, while the foreground is empty, leading to the possibility that the subject of these works may not be the boxers or even their erasure – rather it is the audience. By setting up an unexpected encounter, *The Long Count* brings two types of audience face to face: the people looking at the boxing match and the people looking at the video. This comparison allows us to ask questions about the nature of audience and of spectatorship. Are all audiences the same? Does the size of the audience – whether it's made up of one or many – change the nature of that audience? Does seeing lead to, or confuse, knowing? As an examination of a number of Pfeiffer's works will demonstrate, the subject of viewing and, more importantly, of audience, is one that the artist has returned to over and over again.

»Keep your eye on the ball« is the advice all coaches give to their players in sports, whether in football, baseball, or basketball. In the video work, *John 3:16*, the orange, glowing orb of the basketball is in constant motion; yet by centering it as opposed to allowing it to wander, we are able to keep an eye on it, despite its fluctuating motion of incessant spinning. In order to make this work, Pfeiffer selected dozens of video clips from televised basketball games. He then assembled these disconnected moments and motion-tracked the basketball so that it was stationary, while everything else visible moves.[1] Contrary to our normal experience of a basketball game, Pfeiffer's work restrains the ball, allowing it to spin, but not to travel in space. What this small manipulation achieves, however, is to change the relationship of the subject to the viewer. The traditional structure of the game is reversed. The ball now seems to *control* the players and, by extension, the viewers. The players swarm around it trying to grasp it and throw it, but it never moves and they quickly disappear off camera. In the same way that Copernicus corrected our self-centered misunderstanding about the movement of celestial bodies, Pfeiffer, by hijacking the ball, forces us to consider the larger cultural arena in which the game is being played.[2]

The scenes that comprise *John 3:16* are all found footage, retrieved from broadcasts of different basketball games. By choosing to use only what already existed, as opposed to creating new imagery that might result in the same visual effect, Pfeiffer's video raises questions about the controlling ability of the media and its distribution apparatus. While we think we are viewing a game, in fact what is presented is a particular viewpoint of a game, one that is dictated by the

1. Motion-tracking is an editing process which allows the camera to focus on one detail in the image and use that detail to organize the other information in the video image. This same technique will later be used to create *Morning after the Deluge*.

2. In 1530, Nicolas Copernicus published *De Revolutionibus*, which asserted » ... that the earth rotated on its axis once daily and traveled around the sun once yearly.« In other words, the Earth moved around the Sun. Internet biography search for Copernicus http://www.blupete.com/Literature/Biographies/Science/Copernicus.htm

die wahre Bewegung der Himmelskörper verkannten, weil wir uns selbst für den Mittelpunkt hielten, richtig stellte, zwingt Pfeiffer uns, das größere kulturelle Umfeld zur Kenntnis zu nehmen, innerhalb dessen das Spiel stattfindet, indem er den Ball entführt.[2]

Die Szenen in *John 3:16* beruhen alle auf vorgefundenem Filmmaterial, das den Fernsehaufzeichnungen diverser Basketballspiele entstammt. Durch die Entscheidung, ausschließlich schon existierende Bilder zu verwenden statt neue herzustellen, die möglicherweise dieselbe visuelle Wirkung entfaltet hätten, wirft Pfeiffers Video Fragen hinsichtlich des Kontrollvermögens der Medien und ihres Distributionsapparates auf. Wir meinen, wir sähen ein Spiel, doch in Wirklichkeit präsentiert man uns das Spiel aus einem bestimmten Blickwinkel, der von der Kamera vorgegeben wird. Die Tatsache, dass die Kamera entscheidet, was wir sehen, und damit auch, was wir wissen, wird durch die extreme Bearbeitung hervorgehoben, der Pfeiffer das Material hier unterzieht. Auch der Titel des Werks spielt auf das Thema Kontrolle an. *John 3:16* ist ein offensichtlicher Verweis auf die Bibel, der die komplexe und positive Botschaft des Christentums in einem markanten Spruch zusammenfasst.[3] Zwar ist es verführerisch, den Titel als Hinweis auf einen Zusammenhang zwischen Sport und Religion zu lesen, doch in diesem Fall verweist er auf einen anderen »Entführungsversuch«, nämlich denjenigen der nicht minder medienkundigen religiösen Rechten.[4] Genau in dem Moment, in dem ein Tor oder Korb erzielt wird und die Kamera folglich auf die Torpfosten oder den Korb gerichtet ist, halten bestimmte Zuschauer Schilder mit Bibelzitaten in die Höhe. Aufgrund der Tatsache, dass die Kamera stets dem Ball folgt, vor allem unmittelbar vor einem Korbwurf, gelingt es diesen Zuschauern, ihre Botschaft in die Blickachse des Fernsehpublikums zu schieben. Wie Pfeiffer haben auch sie verstanden, dass das Publikum ein Gefangener ist und derjenige, der die Kontrolle über die Kamera ausübt, entscheidet, was das Publikum wahrnimmt. Doch der entscheidende Unterschied besteht darin, dass Pfeiffers Manipulation offensichtlich und damit dem Betrachter bekannt ist, während dies bei den Manipulationen der religiösen Rechten nicht der Fall ist.

In *Fragments of a Crucifixion (after Francis Bacon)* ist der Ball verschwunden und statt seiner der Spieler in den Mittelpunkt der Aufmerksamkeit gerückt. Mit an den Oberkörper gepressten Armen, einem infolge der physischen Anspannung geschwollenen Bizeps und sinnlos geballten Fäusten rast der anonyme Spieler ständig auf einem leeren Spielfeld hin und her. Nachdem er sich für einen Videoclip mit dem Basketballspieler Larry Johnson entschieden hatte, entfernte Pfeiffer alle Logos und sonstigen identifikatorischen Elemente und loopte dann die nur wenige Sekunden dauernde Handlung, so dass sich Johnsons Bewegung-

camera. The issue of the camera's guidance over what we see and therefore what we know is highlighted by the extreme editing that Pfeiffer performs in this work. The issue of control is also alluded to in the title of the work. *John 3:16*, is an obvious biblical reference that sums up the complex and positive message of Christianity into a sound bite.[3] While it is tempting to read the title as an indicator of a connection between sports and religion, in this context, it indicates another attempted »hijacking«, but this time by the equally media-savvy religious right.[4] Just as a point is about be scored, and thus in the camera's view of goalposts or basketball hoops, certain spectators contrive to hold up signs with this biblical citation. Knowing that the camera will follow the ball, especially as a basket is about to be scored, they are able to insert their message into view of the television audience. Like Pfeiffer, they too understand that the audience is a captive one, and that he who controls the camera shapes what the audience absorbs. The important difference is that Pfeiffer's manipulation is evident and therefore is known to the viewer, while the religious right's is not.

In *Fragment of a Crucifixion (after Francis Bacon)*, the ball is gone and the player has taken its place as the center of attention. In it, a player, rendered anonymous, is constantly pacing back and forth on an empty court, his arms pinned to his sides, with biceps bulging from the strain of his physical exertion and his hands uselessly clenched. After selecting a clip of the basketball player, Larry Johnson, Pfeiffer erased all logos and other identifying references and then looped the few seconds of action so that Johnson's movements are endlessly repeated. We quickly realize we are not the only viewers of this scene of impotent rage, and in fact the audience that fills the arena to capacity is busy recording and seemingly tormenting Johnson with their camera flashes, which incessantly push and pull him from left to right. These camera flashes, which operate more like gunshots, redirect his movements as he attempts to evade them, leading one critic to describe Johnson as »a hunted animal« being pursued by the unrelenting camera shots of the crowd.[5] As such, the audience now controls Johnson's movements, thus redirecting our attention from the center to the periphery. In other words, through a series of technical manipulations, an inversion occurs in which the spectators *control* the action on the court, rather than *follow* it.

In *The Long Count* videos, the athletes – in this case the boxers – are gone and the audience has taken its place as the center of our attention.[6] Exploiting the full capabilities of digital technology to rewrite the truth – in a way that photography could only dream of – Pfeiffer erases the balletic movements of the most graceful of boxers, Muhammad Ali, and his lumbering opponent, Joe Frazier in *The Long Count (Thrilla in Manila)* and replaces them with a shimmering shadow play

2. 1530 veröffentlichte Nikolaus Kopernikus sein Werk *De Revolutionibus*, in dem er erklärte, »...dass die Erde sich einmal täglich um ihre eigene Achse dreht und ein Jahr lang um die Sonne kreist«. Mit anderen Worten: Die Erde dreht sich um die Sonne und nicht umgekehrt. Vgl. die Kopernikus-Biografie im Internet unter http://www.blupete.com/Literature/Biographies/Science/Copernicus.htm

3. Johannes 3, 16: »Also hat Gott die Welt geliebt, dass er seinen eingeborenen Sohn gab, auf dass alle, die an ihn glauben, nicht verloren werden, sondern das ewige Leben haben.«

4. In einem Gespräch mit dem Autor verwendete Pfeiffer das Wort »Entführung« (Highjacking) zur Beschreibung des Verhaltens derjenigen Besucher von Sportveranstaltungen, die während der verschiedenen Spiele derartige Schilder hochhielten.

3. *John 3:16*, »For God so loved the world that he gave his only Son, that whoever believes in him should not perish but have eternal life.«

4. In a conversation with the author, Pfeiffer used the word »hijacking« to describe the action of those sports viewers who held up these signs at different games.

5. Roberta Smith, »Paul Pfeiffer«, New York Times, 15 December, 2000), p. E41

en endlos wiederholen. Sehr schnell realisieren wir, dass wir nicht die einzigen Betrachter dieser Szene ohnmächtiger Wut sind, sondern dass die Sportarena bis zum letzten Platz gefüllt ist und die Zuschauer damit beschäftigt sind, Johnson mit den Blitzen ihrer Kameras, die ihn immer wieder von links nach rechts ziehen, aufzunehmen, aber offenbar auch zu quälen. Dass diese Kamerablitze, die an Mündungsfeuer erinnern, Johnsons Bewegungen beeinflussen, zeigt sich daran, dass er ihnen auszuweichen versucht, weswegen sich eine Kritikerin an ein »gejagtes Tier« erinnert fühlte, das von den erbarmungslosen Kameraschüssen der Masse verfolgt wird.[5] Das Publikum also kontrolliert Johnsons Bewegungen und lenkt unsere Aufmerksamkeit vom Zentrum auf die Peripherie. Oder anders gesagt, durch eine Reihe technischer Manipulationen kommt es zu einer Umkehrung, infolge derer die Zuschauer das Geschehen auf dem Spielfeld kontrollieren statt ihm lediglich zu folgen.

In den *The Long Count* Videos sind die Athleten, in diesem Fall die Boxer, verschwunden, und stattdessen ist das Publikum in den Mittelpunkt unseres Interesses gerückt.[6] Indem er die Fähigkeiten der digitalen Technologie voll ausschöpft, um die Wahrheit umzuschreiben – und dies auf eine Weise tut, von der die Fotografie nur träumen kann –, tilgt Pfeiffer die ballettartigen Bewegungen des anmutigsten aller Boxer und seines schwerfälligen Gegners – Joe Frazier in *The Long Count (Thrilla in Manila)* – und ersetzt sie durch ein schimmerndes Schattenspiel von kurzen Geraden und Schlägen. Und dennoch sind diese Nicht-Figuren nach wie vor zu erkennen, denn ihre Konturen tanzen durch den Ring. Freilich lohnt es sich kaum, sie zu beobachten, denn es ist klar, dass unser Interesse auf die Figuren im Publikum gelenkt werden soll. Die gebannte Aufmerksamkeit, die auf vielen dieser Gesichter geschrieben steht, verdeutlicht, dass es dem von der Kamera aufgezeichneten Publikum im Gegensatz zu den Betrachtern von Pfeiffers Video keine Schwierigkeiten bereitet, das wahrzunehmen, was wir nur mühsam erahnen können. Wenn in dem hiermit vergleichbaren Video *The Long Count (Rumble in the Jumble)* jemand im Publikum aufsteht (was häufig vorkommt), tut er dies, um über den Kopf eines anderen Zuschauers hinwegzusehen. Und wenn andere Zuschauer von ihren Sitzen aufspringen und schreien und Beifall rufen, dann haben sie mit Sicherheit jenen Schlag gesehen, den wir, wie Alis Gegner George Foreman, nicht einmal kommen sahen.[7]

Auch in *Morning after the Deluge,* Pfeiffers letztem Werk, ist Schauen beziehungsweise Sehen das Thema, obwohl diesmal sogar das Publikum aus dem Bild entfernt wurde. Hier wird das Betrachten eines Sonnenunter- oder aufgangs, also etwas, das jeder schon mindestens einmal erlebt hat, repliziert, doch weder so, wie man es selbst jemals gesehen hat, noch auf eine auf natürlichem Wege sicht-

of jabs and punches. These non-figures, however, are still perceptible as their outlines dance around the ring. Watching them ultimately offers little reward, as the figures we should be focusing on are those in the audience. Unlike the viewers of Pfeiffer's video, the recorded audience has no trouble seeing what we must strain to make out, evidenced by the rapt attention noticeable on many of their faces. In the related video, *The Long Count (Rumble in the Jungle)*, when a member of the audience stands up (as they often do) it is to see over the head of a fellow spectator; when others jump out of their seats and yell and cheer, they have certainly seen the punch that we, like Ali's opponent George Foreman, never saw coming.[7]

Morning after the Deluge, Pfeiffer's latest work, once again takes looking or viewing as its subject, though this time even the audience has been eliminated. The act of looking at a sunset or sunrise – something every person has done at least once – is replicated, but in neither a way that has ever been seen before, nor that can be seen with natural vision. Pfeiffer recorded both a sunset and a sunrise from the beaches in Provincetown, Massachusetts, a location he chose because it allowed him to film both movements of the sun over water. Later in the studio, he spliced the two pieces of film, flipping one, so that the horizons met and became one. By motion-tracking the sun and keeping it centered in the frame (much like the basketball in *John 3:16*) our traditional frames of references – the landscape and the horizon – are eliminated. This sun neither sets nor rises. At first, as we view this piece, nothing seems to happen. Eventually, a glimmering, pulsating line – the two horizons spliced together – starts to descend from the top of the screen. As this line makes its way to the centered sun and then continues on down, a bird occasionally flies through the sky, appearing only long enough to startle the viewer.

In this latest work, the sun remains fixed in space, while the world circles around it: which is, of course, the way it actually is. From our vantage point – standing in one place and seeing the sun set – we are still tempted to believe, as did people for many centuries, that the sun moves and the earth is stationary.[8] Vision and knowledge are two different things. In *Morning after the Deluge,* all the representations of looking explored in previous videos – the frozen ball, the controlled player, and the audience – have been stripped away. We are now left with only the familiar act of looking, but without the comfort that we normally expect from it.

In *Morning after the Deluge,* important questions about vision and its connection to knowledge are raised: questions that are no less pertinent today than they were in Goethe's or Copernicus' time, questions touching upon the contemporary conditions of spectatorship. All the works discussed so far, with the important exception of *Morning after the Deluge,* are primarily images of spectacles that are normally con-

5. Roberta Smith, »Paul Pfeiffer«, *New York Times*, 15. Dezember 2000, S. E41

6. Eine andere Lesart der Bedeutung der Tilgung der Hauptfigur bietet Dominic Molon, »Corporealities«, in: *Paul Pfeiffer*, Ausst. Kat. MIT List Visual Center, Cambridge and Museum of Contemporary Art, Chicago, Chicago, 2003, S. 17

7. Ali schlug George Foreman in der 8. Runde des Kampfes um die Weltmeisterschaft im Schwergewicht, der 1974 in Kinshasa, Zaire, stattfand. Ich verdanke diese Information der eMail-Korrespondenz mit Frazer Ward, einem Kunsthistoriker und ehemaligen Amateur-Schwergewichtsboxer.

6. For another reading of the significance of the removal of the main figure, see Dominic Molon, »Corporealities«, in *Paul Pfeiffer*, exhibition catalogue MIT List Visual Arts Center, Cambridge and Museum of Contemporary Art, Chicago, Chicago, 2003, p. 17

7. Ali knocked out George Foreman in the 8th round of the World Heavyweight Championship match held in Kinshasa, Zaire, in 1974. From an E-Mail correspondence with Frazer Ward, art historian and former amateur heavyweight boxer.

8. »Of all discoveries and opinions, none may have exerted a greater effect on the human spirit than the doctrine of Copernicus. The world had scarcely become known as round and complete in itself when it was asked to waive the tremendous privilege of being the center of the universe. Never,

bare Weise. Mittels der Kamera hat Pfeiffer am Strand von Provincetown, Massachusetts, einen Sonnenuntergang und einen Sonnenaufgang aufgenommen. Er wählte diesen Ort, weil er hier beide Phänomene oberhalb der Wasseroberfläche filmen konnte. Später im Studio klebte er die beiden Filme aneinander, wobei er den einen umdrehte, so dass die Horizonte einander berührten und zu einem einzigen verschmolzen. Dadurch dass er die Sonne mittels des Motion-Track-Verfahrens dauerhaft im Zentrum des Bildes platzierte (ähnlich wie bei dem Basketball in *John 3:16*), wurden unsere traditionellen Bezugsgrößen – die Landschaft und der Horizont – eliminiert. Diese Sonne geht weder unter noch auf. Betrachtet man das Bild, scheint zunächst nichts zu geschehen. Doch allmählich beginnt sich eine schimmernde pulsierende Linie – die beiden aneinander geklebten Horizonte – vom oberen Rand der Leinwand herab zu schieben. Während diese Linie sich auf die Sonne in der Mitte zubewegt und von dort nach unten weiterzieht, fliegt ab und zu ein Vogel durch das Bild, und ist dort genau so lang zu sehen, um beim Betrachter ein Gefühl der Verblüffung hervorzurufen.
In diesem letzten Werk bleibt die Sonne im Raum fixiert, während die Welt sich um sie herum dreht; das heißt, sie verhält sich genau so, wie sie dies auch in Wirklichkeit tut. Von unserem Standpunkt aus – wir stehen an einem Ort und sehen, wie die Sonne untergeht –, tendieren wir noch immer zu der Meinung, die Sonne bewege sich und die Erde stünde fest, wie dies die Menschen viele Jahrhunderte lang glaubten.[8] Sehen und Wissen sind zwei verschiedene Dinge. In *Morning after the Deluge* wurden alle Darstellungen des Sehens, die in früheren Videos erkundet wurden – der auf der Stelle festgefrorene Ball, der kontrollierte Spieler und das Publikum – beseitigt. Alles was uns bleibt ist der vertraute Akt des Sehens, doch ohne den Trost, den wir normalerweise daraus beziehen.
Morning after the Deluge wirft wichtige Fragen hinsichtlich des Sehens und seines Zusammenhangs mit dem Wissen auf, Fragen, die heute nicht weniger relevant sind als zu Goethes oder Kopernikus' Zeit, Fragen, die an die zeitgenössischen Bedingungen des Zuschauerseins rühren. Alle bisher besprochenen Werke, mit der wichtigen Ausnahme von *Morning after the Deluge,* sind primär Bilder von Spektakeln, die normalerweise zeitgleich von Massen von Zuschauern konsumiert werden. Sowohl Basketballspiele als auch Boxkämpfe sind extrem orchestrierte Ereignisse, bei denen das Publikum in den Arenen zu einem zentralen Bestandteil wird. Doch in Pfeiffers Videos, in denen das Publikum selbst das Thema ist, blickt ein Publikum des einen auf ein Publikum der vielen. Diese Manipulation verwandelt ein passives Massenspektakel in eine Gelegenheit aktiven Sehens.
Den täglichen Sonnenauf- oder untergang betrachtet man normalerweise alleine oder in Gesellschaft eines geliebten Menschen, jedoch nicht in Gesell-

sumed simultaneously by masses of viewers. Both basketball games and boxing matches are highly orchestrated events in which the audience, in the arenas, becomes a central component. In Pfeiffer's videos, however, where the subject is audience, an audience of one gazes upon an audience of many. This manipulation transforms a passive spectacle of mass participation into an opportunity for active viewing.
The viewing of the sun rising and setting on a daily basis is an activity normally done either by oneself or in the company of a loved one, but not in a crowd. Tellingly, however, *Morning after the Deluge* is a projection. This very large image is set up by Pfeiffer to be seen by many people at the same time. What was normally a contemplative exercise performed in isolation, is now an orchestrated event to be seen in the presence of many viewers. Once again, Pfeiffer's consistent playful inversions are evident: a sporting spectacle becomes an intimate depiction of active viewing, while the private act of watching the sun rise is rendered into an alien, yet instructive, phenomenon that can only be appreciated en masse. While the connection between vision and knowledge has been called into question before – by other artists, philosophers, and scientists – it is useful to do so repeatedly, for this uncoupling is both distressing and not obvious. This lesson, which one can glean from Pfeiffer's work, has been updated to deal with contemporary problems, such as the increasing control the media has over what we see and our distressing willingness to accept at face-value the imagery we consume.

8. Goethe bemerkte dazu in seiner Farbenlehre: »... unter allen Entdeckungen und Überzeugungen möchte nichts eine größere Wirkung auf den menschlichen Geist hervorgebracht haben als die Lehre des Kopernikus. Kaum war die Welt als rund anerkannt und in sich selbst abgeschlossen, so sollte sie auf das ungeheure Vorrecht Verzicht tun, der Mittelpunkt des Weltalls zu sein. Vielleicht ist noch nie eine größere Forderung an die Menschheit geschehen: denn was ging nicht alles durch diese Anerkennung in Dunst und Rauch auf: ein zweites Paradies, eine Welt der Unschuld, Dichtkunst und Frömmigkeit, das Zeugnis der Sinne, die Überzeugung eines poetisch-religiösen Glaubens; kein Wunder, dass man dies alles nicht wollte fahren lassen, dass man sich auf alle Weise einer solchen Lehre entgegensetzte, die denjenigen, der sie annahm, zu einer bisher unbekannten, ja ungeahnten Denkfreiheit und Grossheit der Gesinnung berechtigte und aufforderte.«

perhaps, was a greater demand made on mankind – for by this admission so many things vanished in mist and smoke! What became of our Eden, our world of innocence, piety and poetry; the testimony of the senses; the conviction of a poetic – religious faith? No wonder his contemporaries did not wish to let all this go and offered every possible resistance to a doctrine which in its converts authorized and demanded a freedom of view and greatness of thought so far unknown, indeed not even dreamed of.« From Johann Wolfgang von Goethe's, Colour Theory

schaft. Doch bezeichnenderweise handelt es sich bei *Morning after the Deluge* um eine Projektion. Dieses sehr große Bild wurde von Pfeifer so angelegt, dass es von vielen Menschen gleichzeitig gesehen werden kann. Das, was normalerweise eine kontemplative, isoliert praktizierte Übung war, ist nun ein orchestriertes Ereignis, das in Gegenwart vieler Betrachter wahrgenommen werden soll. Einmal mehr treten Pfeiffers konsequente spielerische Umkehrungen hier deutlich zu Tage: Ein Sportspektakel wird eine intime Darstellung aktiven Schauens, während das private Betrachten des Sonnenaufgangs zu einem fremdartigen, aber instruktiven Phänomen wird, das nur in der Masse wirklich angemessen gewürdigt werden kann. Obgleich die Verbindung von Sehen und Wissen schon früher in Frage gestellt wurde – von anderen Künstlern, Philosophen und Wissenschaftlern – ist es sinnvoll, sie immer wieder zu hinterfragen, denn diese Loslösung ist beides, beunruhigend und keineswegs offensichtlich zugleich. Diese Lehre, die man aus Pfeiffers Werken ziehen kann, wurde aktualisiert, um auch zeitgenössischen Problemen gerecht zu werden, etwa das der zunehmenden Kontrolle, die die Medien über das ausüben, was wir sehen, und unsere beunruhigende Bereitschaft die Bilder, die wir konsumieren, für bare Münze zu nehmen.

Übersetzung aus dem Englischen: Nikolaus G. Schneider

STEFANO BASILICO ist Kurator an der University Art Collection der New School University in New York und beigeordneter Kurator für Zeitgenössische Kunst am Milwaukee Art Museum, Milwaukee, Wisconsin. Seine jüngsten Ausstellungsprojekte umfassen unter anderem *Currents 31: Robert Melee* und *OnSite: Liam Gillick* am Milwaukee Art Museum. Sowie *CUT/Film*, das Ende des Jahres als »Found Object« am Museum of Contemporary Art in North Miami eröffnet wird. Er lebt und arbeitet in New York.

Der Essay »Paul Pfeiffer - Disturbing Vision« von Stefano Basilico wurde für die Publikation *Paul Pfeiffer* in Auftrag gegeben, die Teil der offiziellen Präsentation der U.S.A. auf der Internationalen Biennale von Kairo 2003 war. Diese Ausstellung wurde von der künstlerischen Ko-Kommissarin Holly Block, Executive Director of Art in General in New York, und Jane Farver, Direktorin des Massachusetts Institute of Art's List Visual Arts Center in Cambridge, Massachusetts, organisiert.

STEFANO BASILICO is Curator of the University Art Collection at New School University, New York, and Adjunct Curator of Contemporary Art at the Milwaukee Art Museum, Milwaukee, Wisconsin. His most recent exhibition projects include *Currents 31: Robert Melee* and *OnSite: Liam Gillick* at the Milwaukee Art Museum; and opening in early winter *CUT/Film* as Found Object at Museum of Contemporary Art, North Miami. He lives and works in New York.

The essay »Paul Pfeiffer, Disturbing Vision« by Stefano Basilico was commissioned for the publication *Paul Pfeiffer* as part of the official United States presentation at the 2003 International Biennale of Cairo. This exhibition was organized by co-commissioners Holly Block of Art, Executive Director of Art in General in New York, New York, and Jane Farver, Director of the Massachusetts Institute of Art's List Visual Arts Center in Cambridge, Massachusetts.

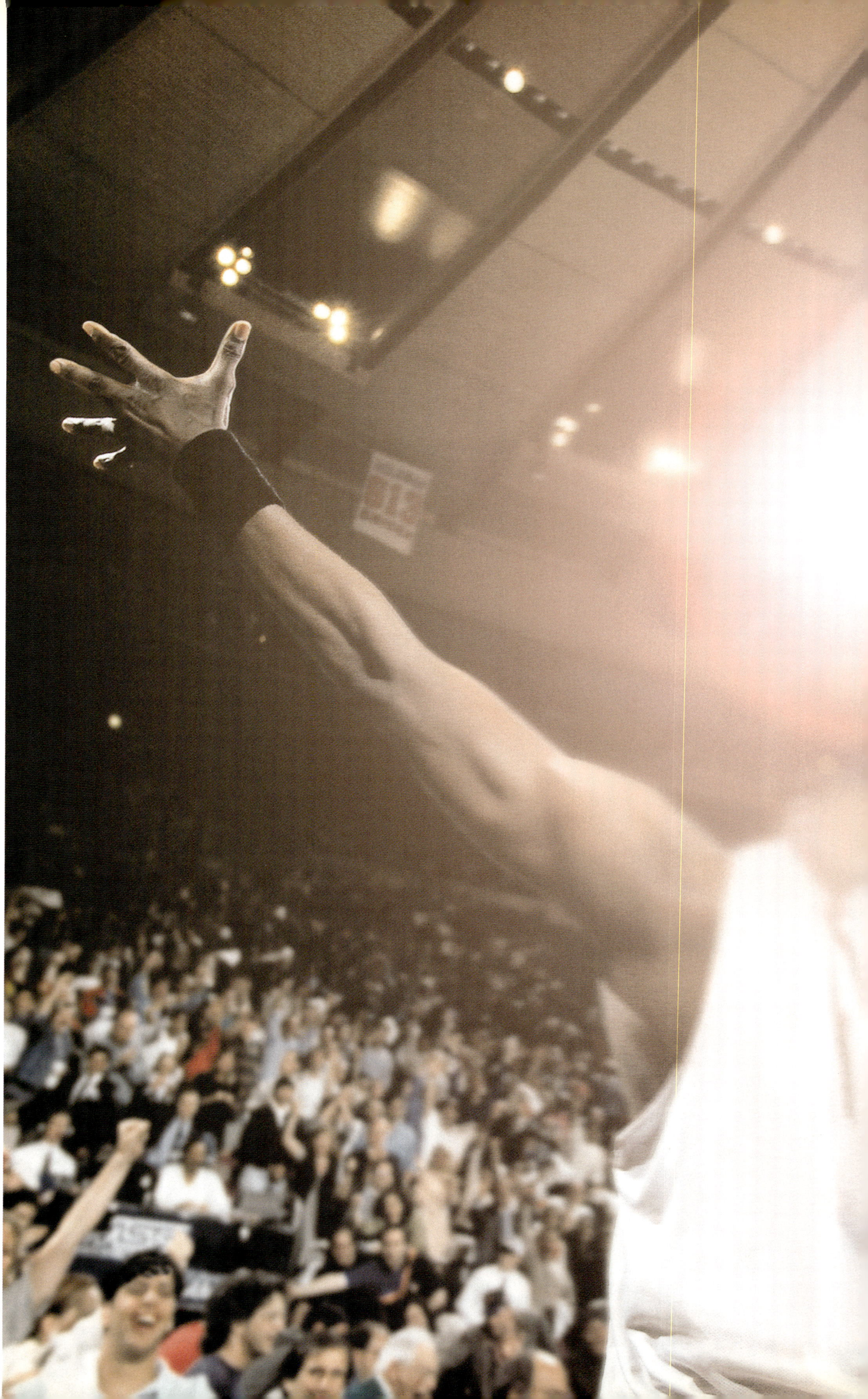

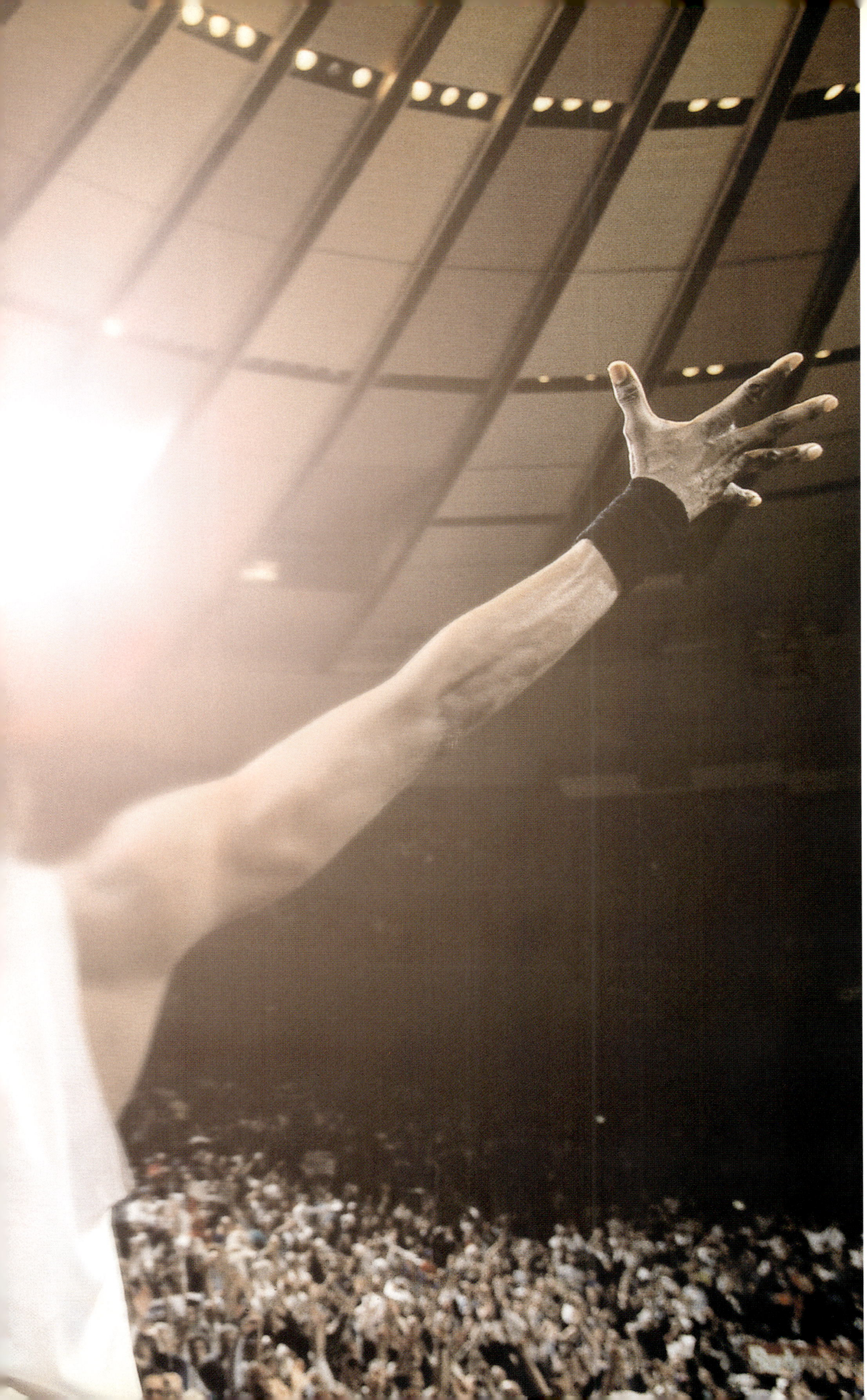

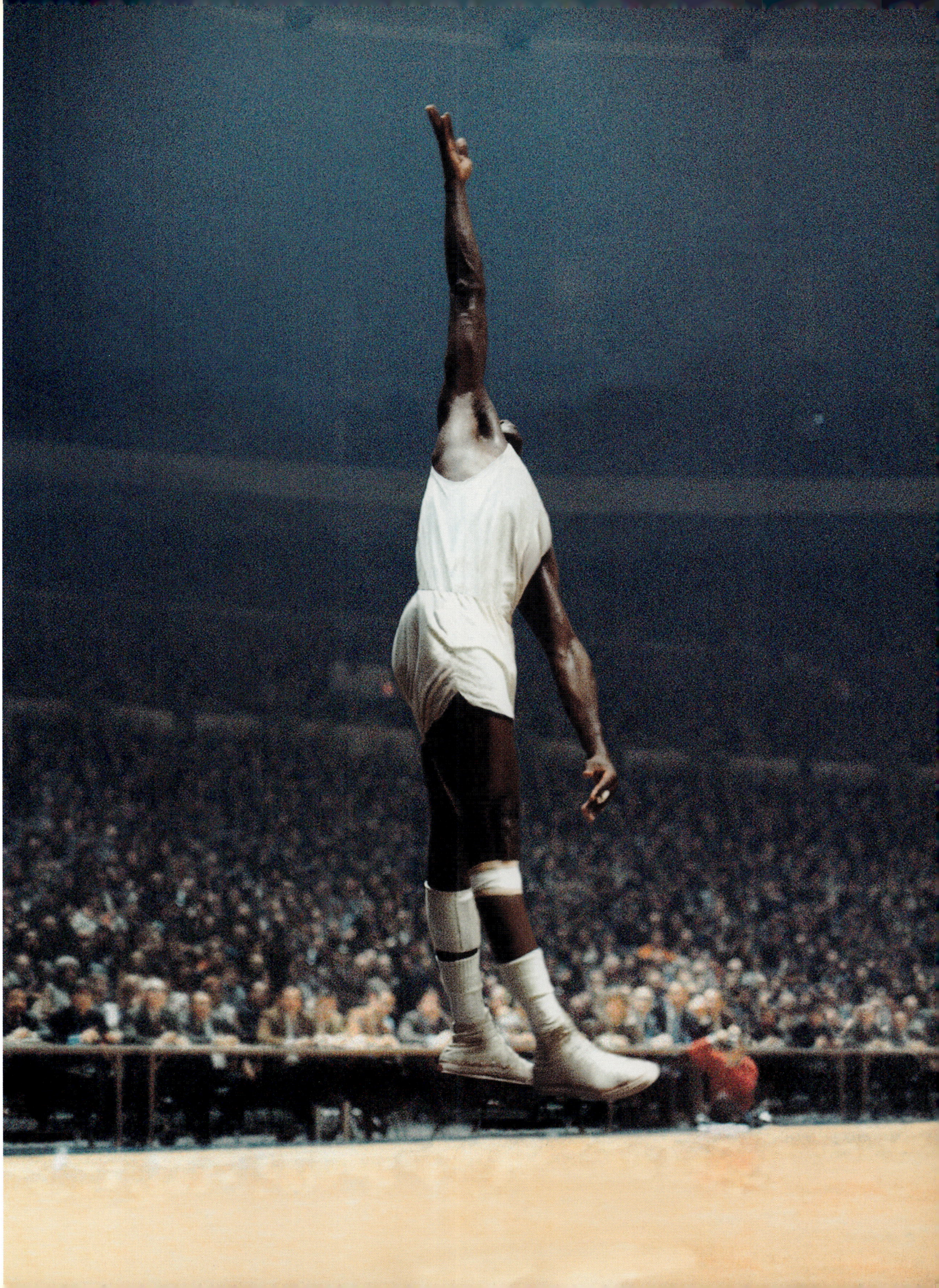

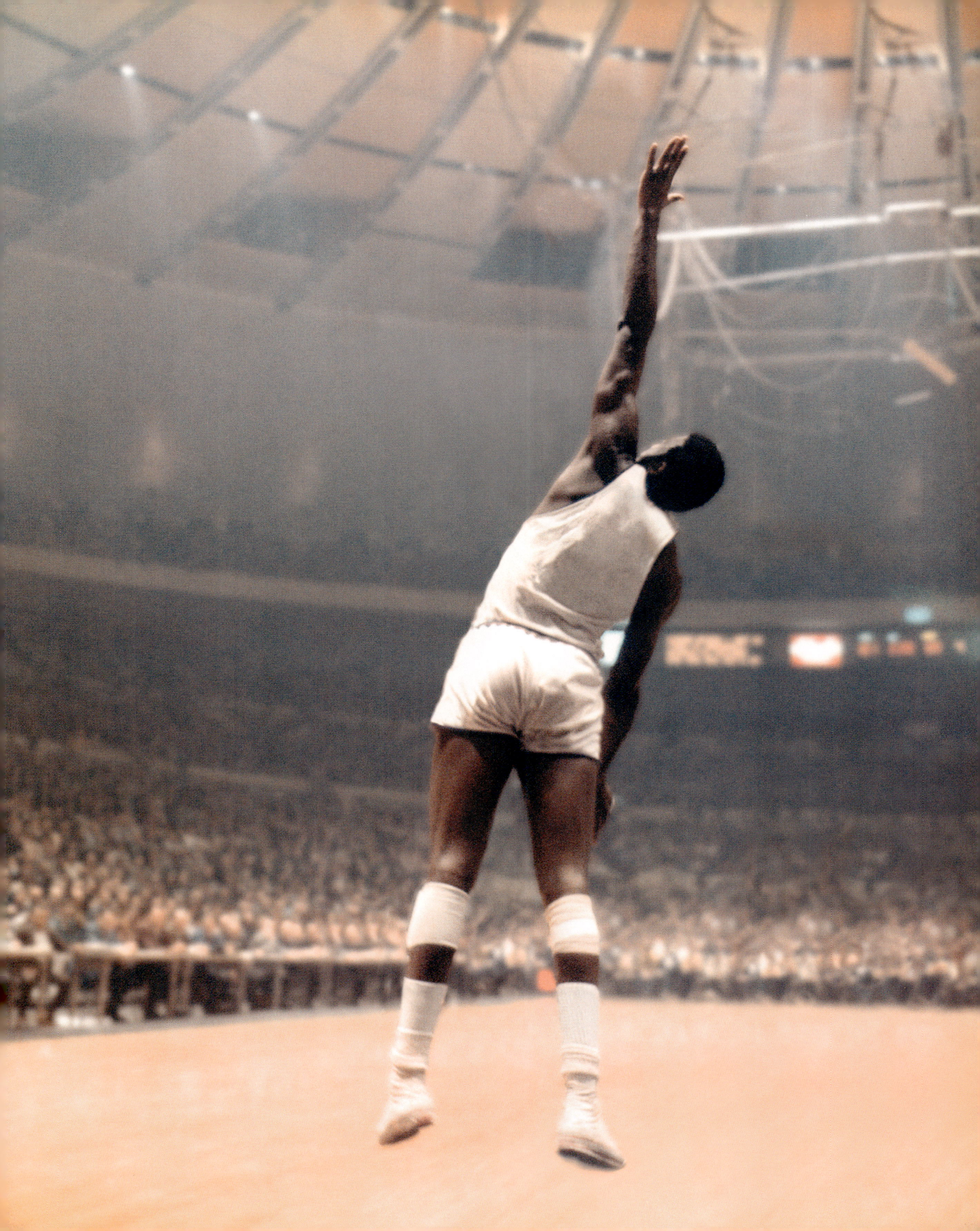

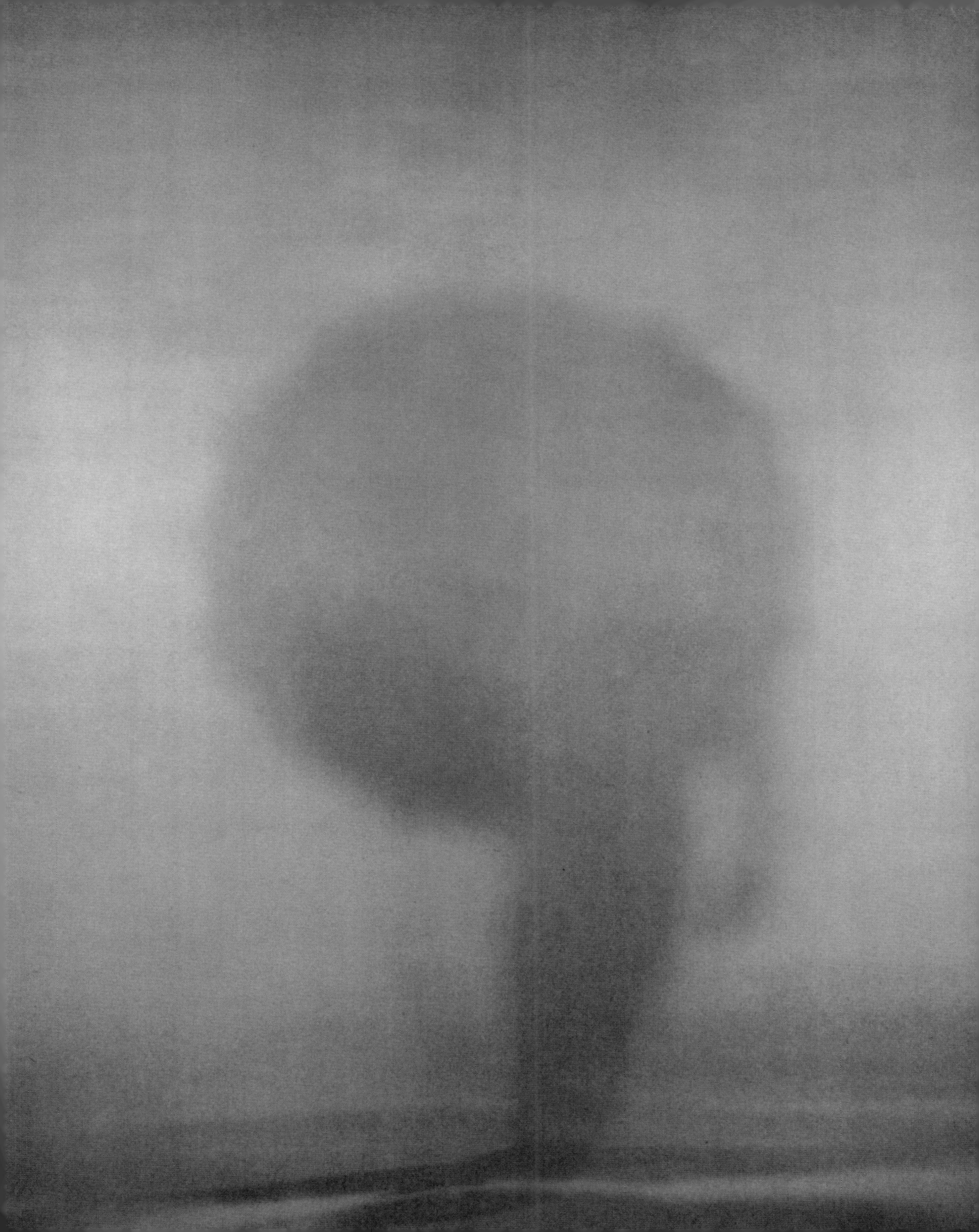

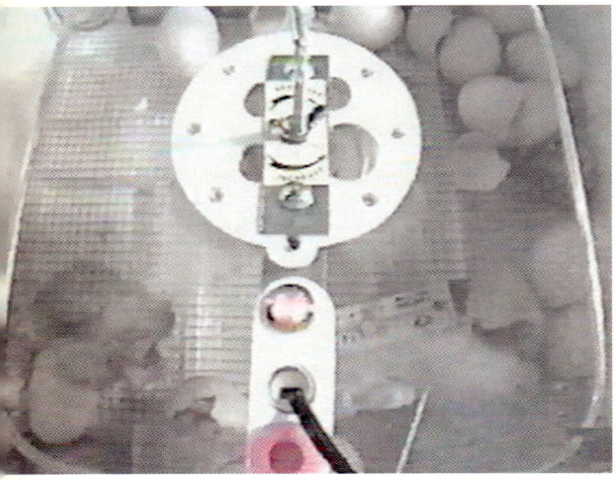
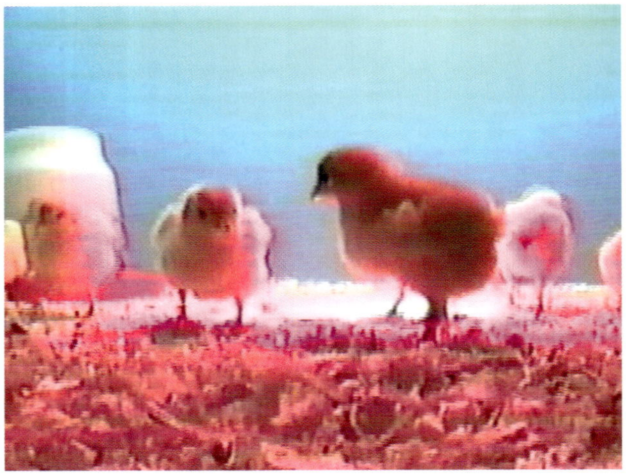
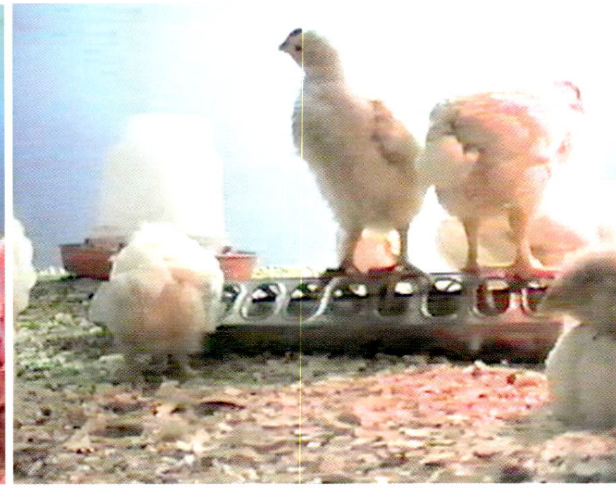
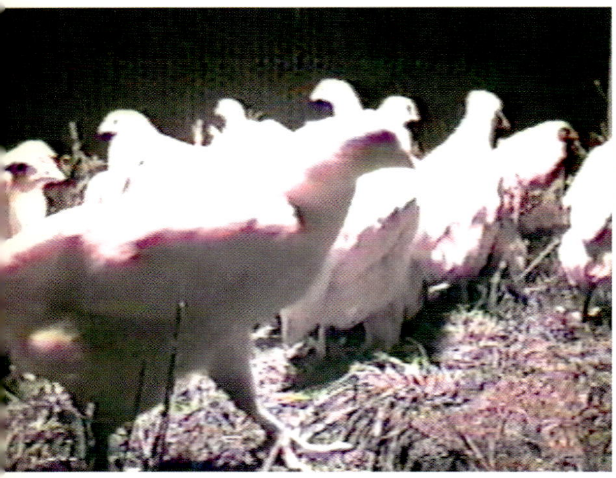
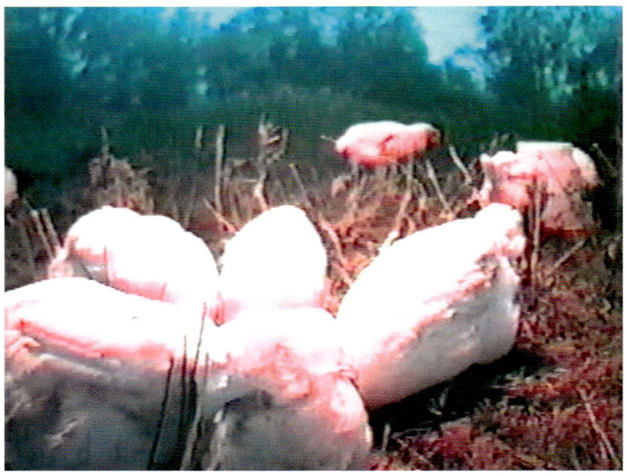
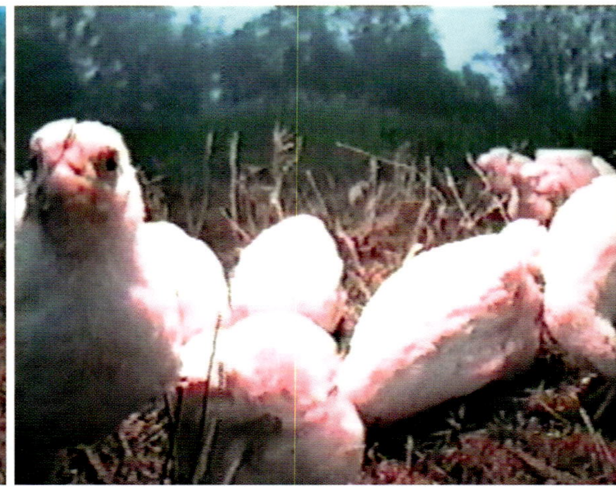
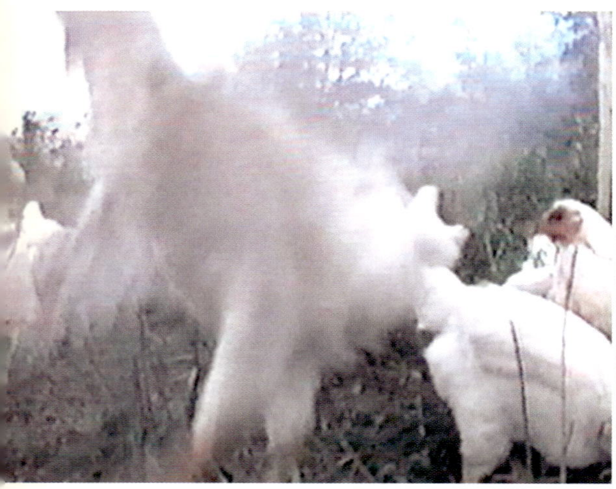
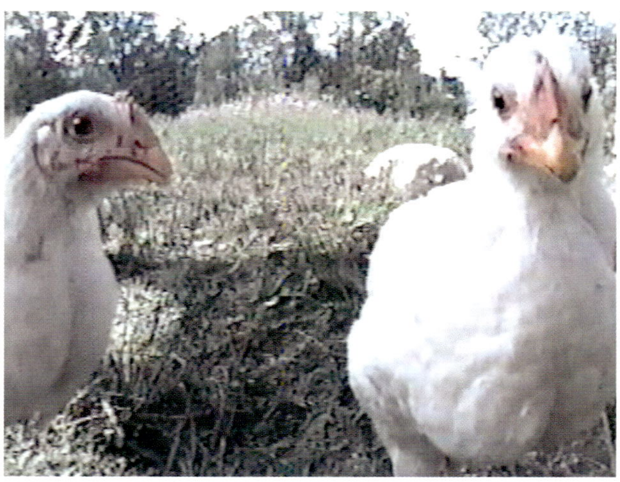
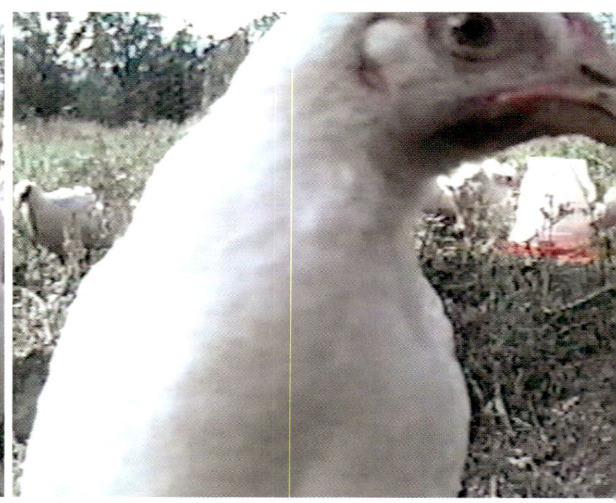

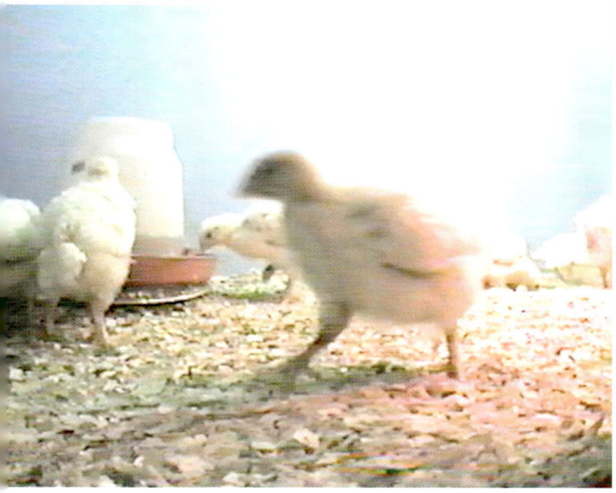
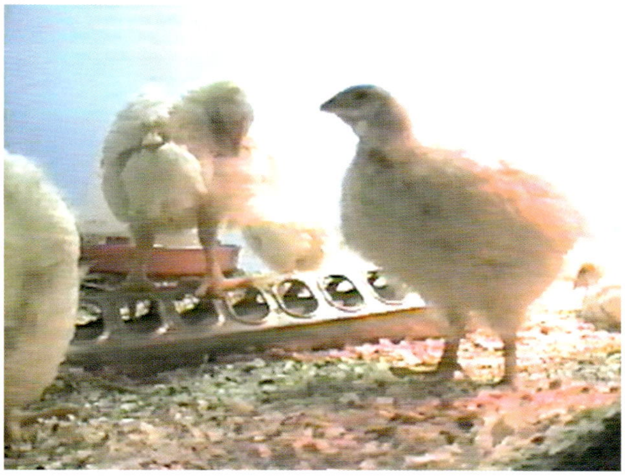
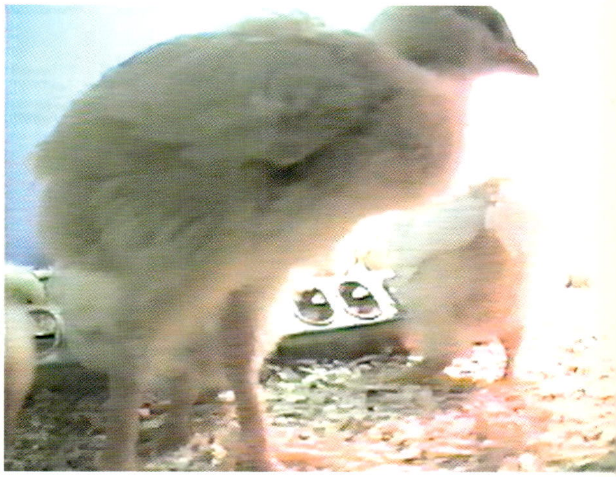
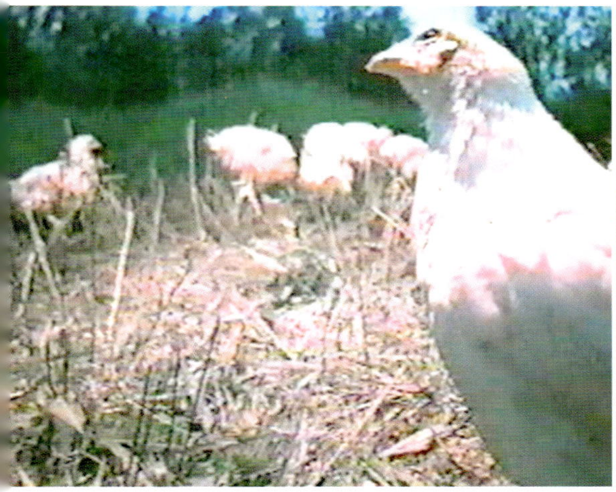
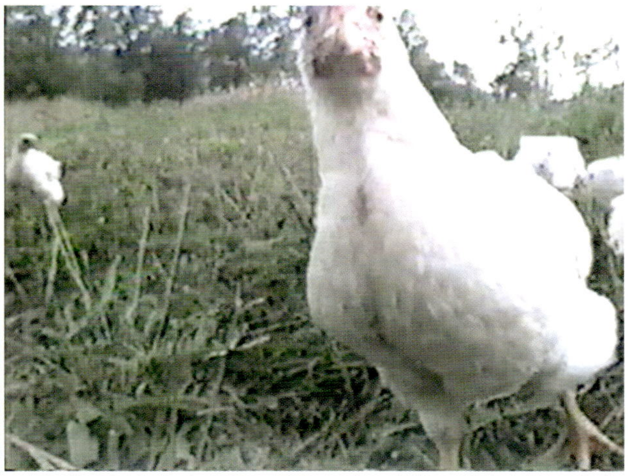
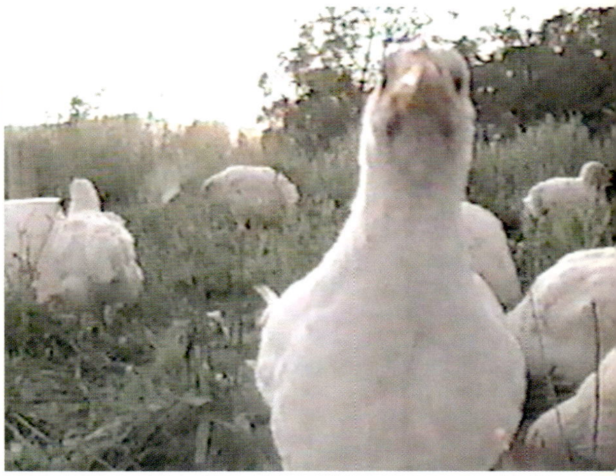
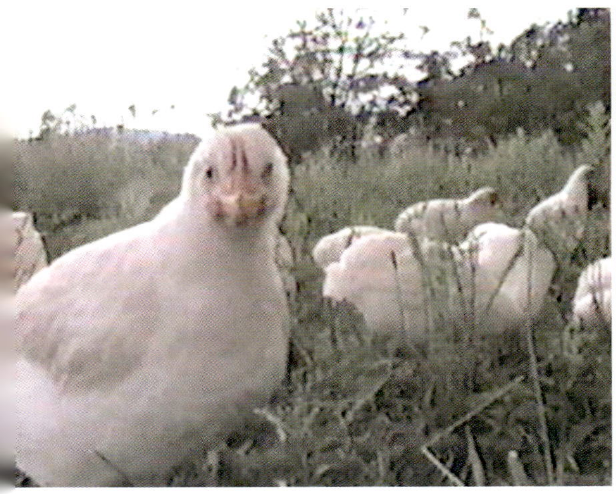
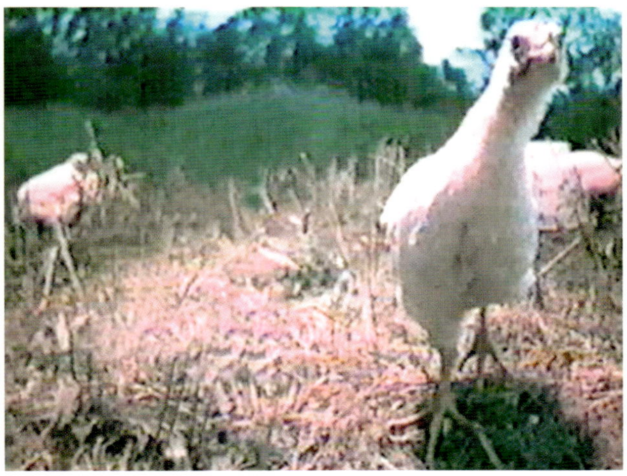
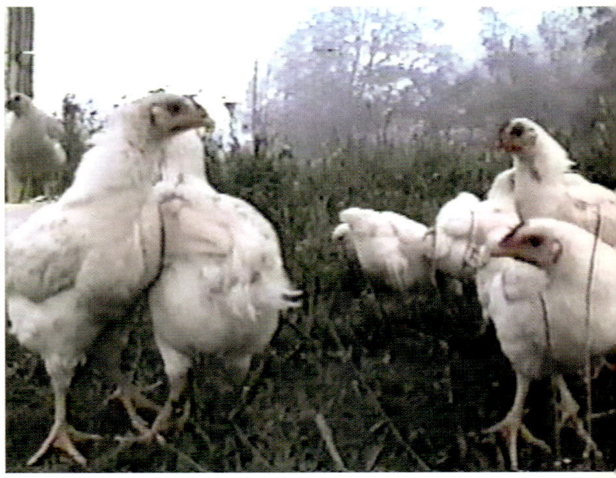

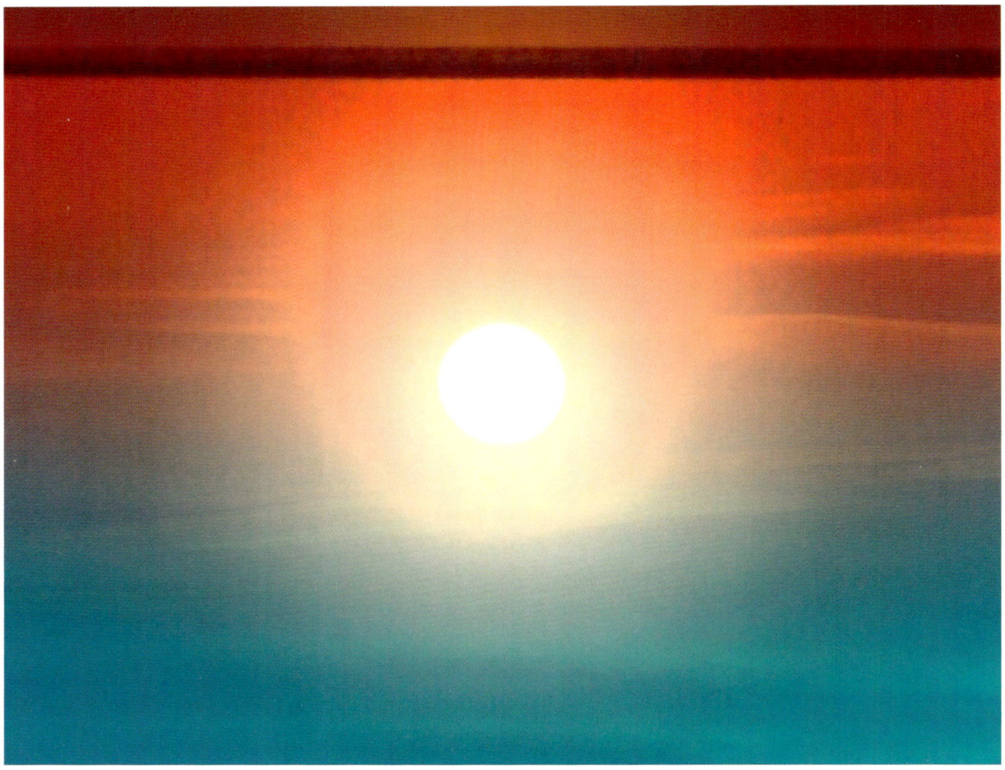

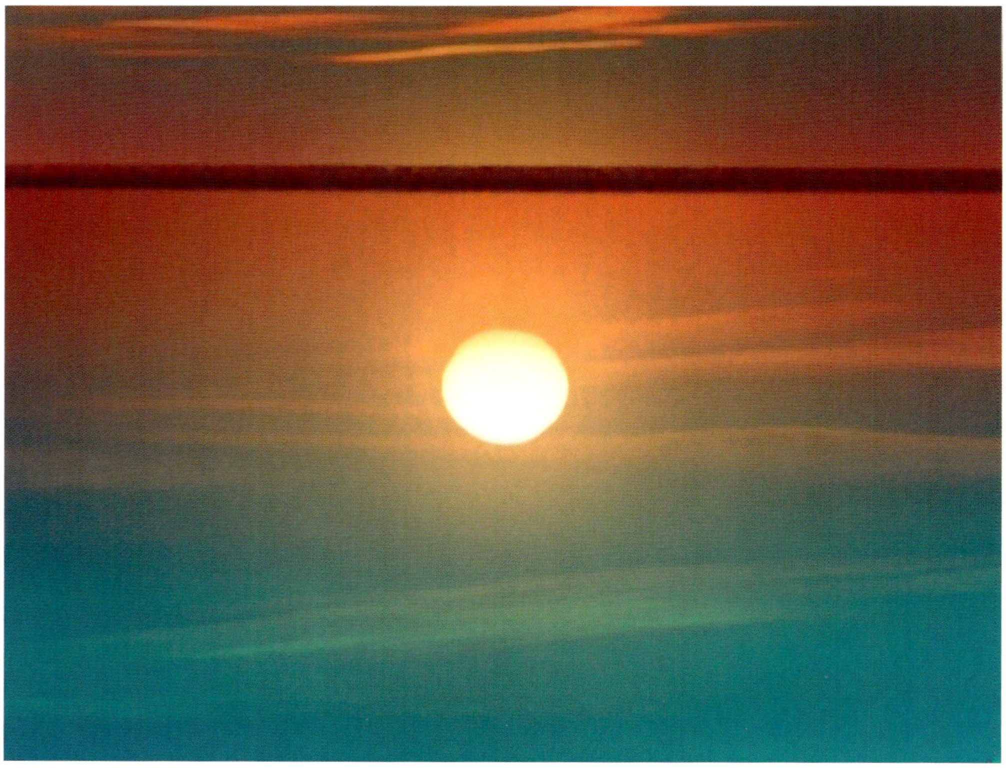

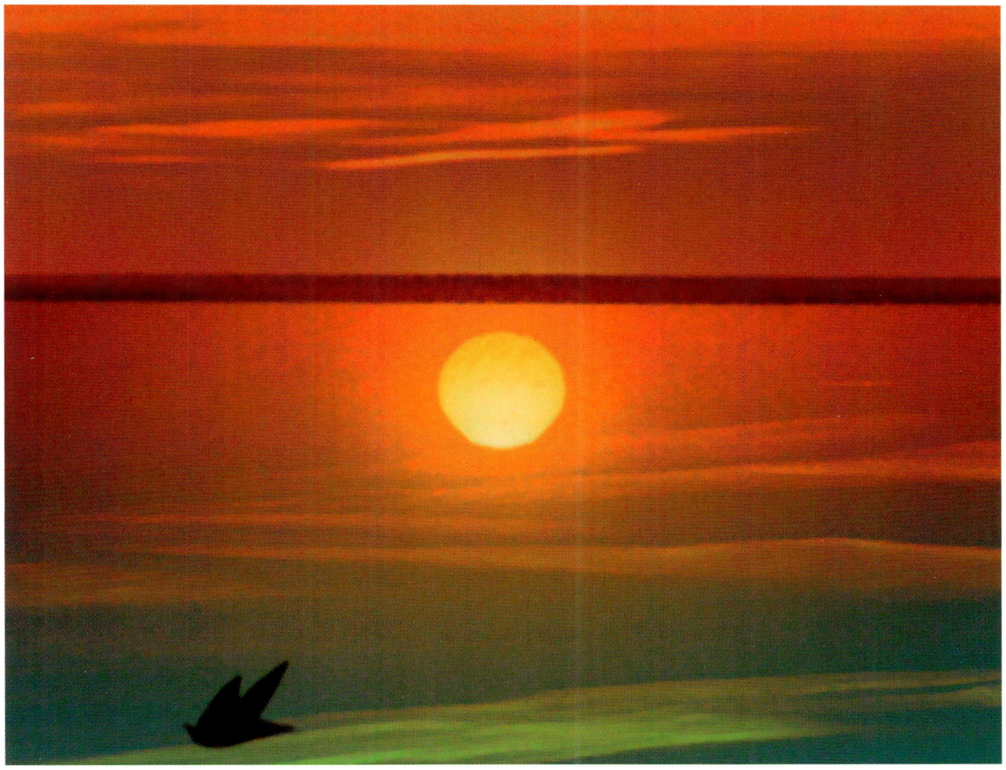

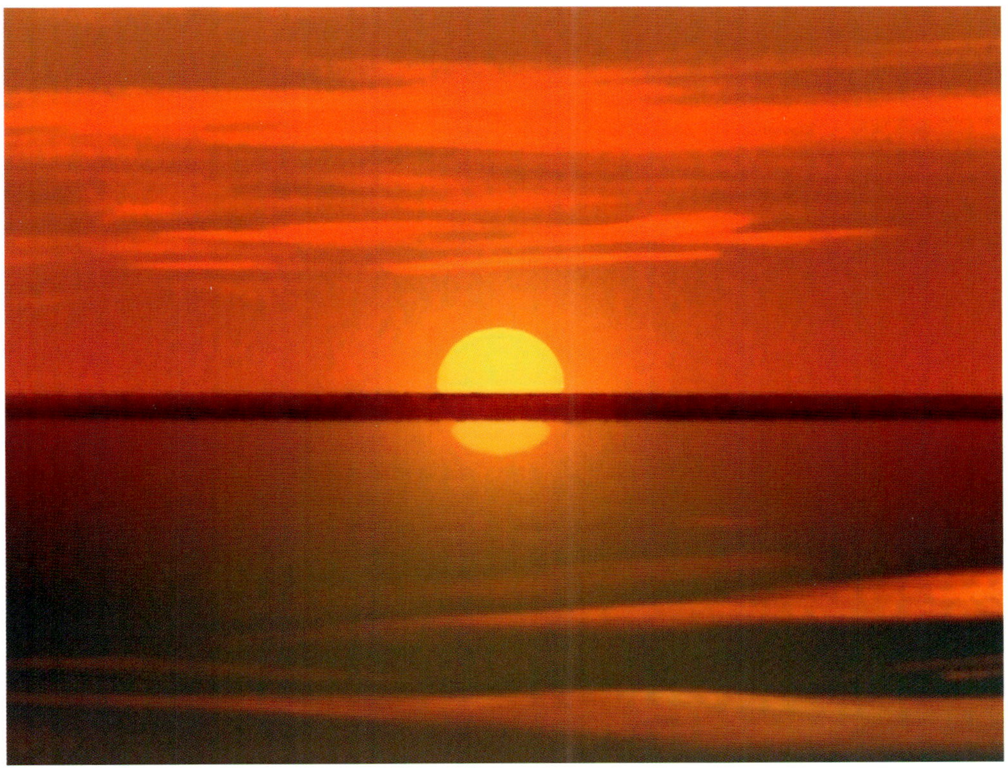

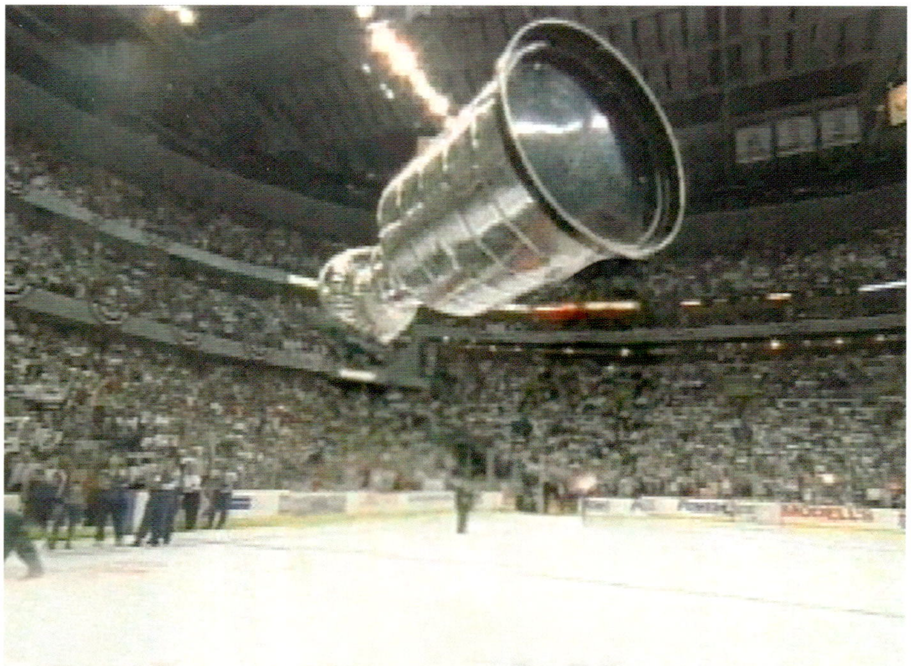

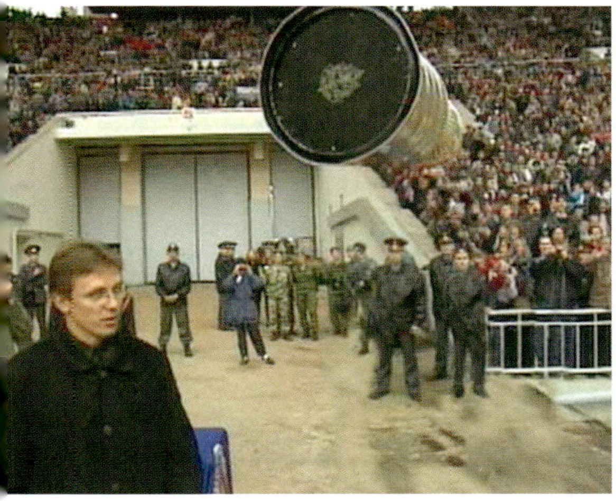
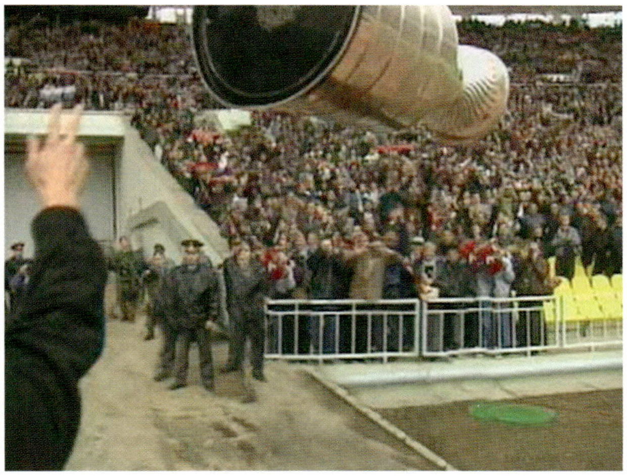
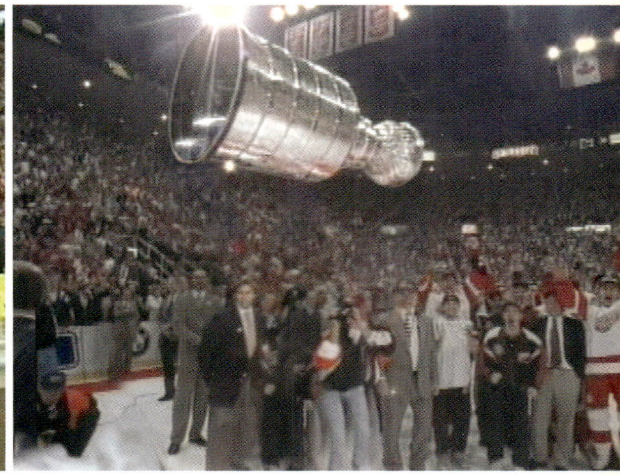
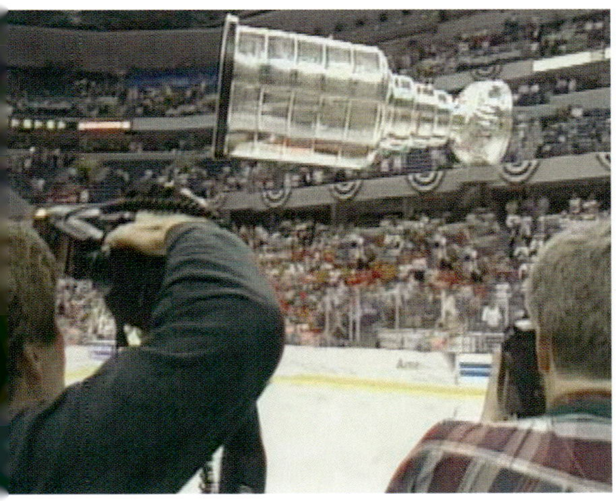
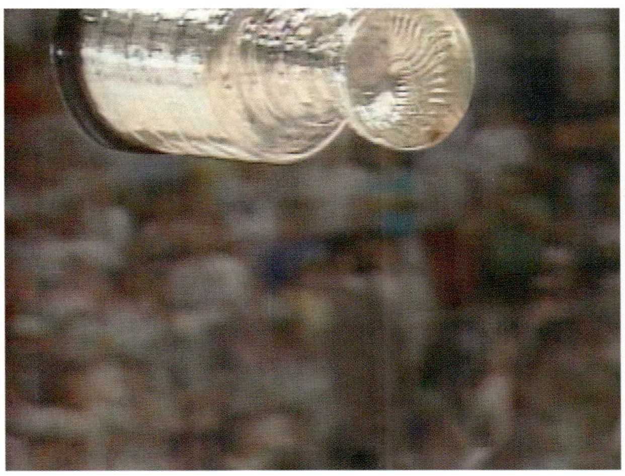
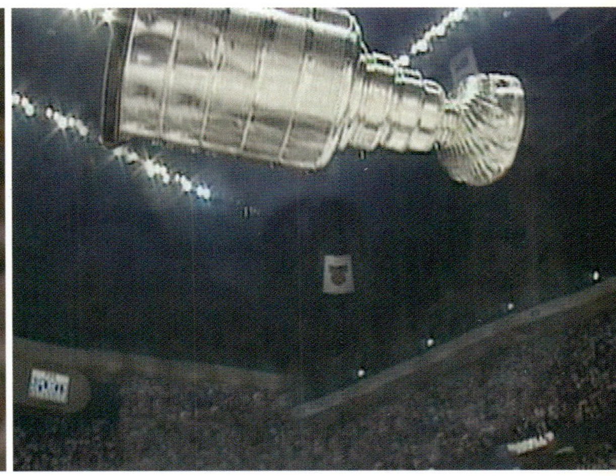
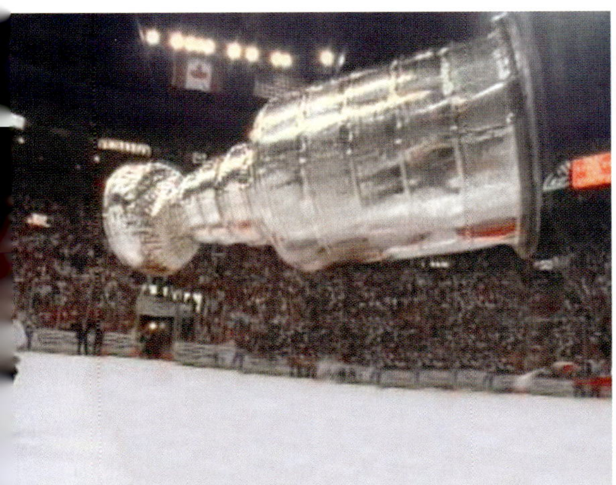
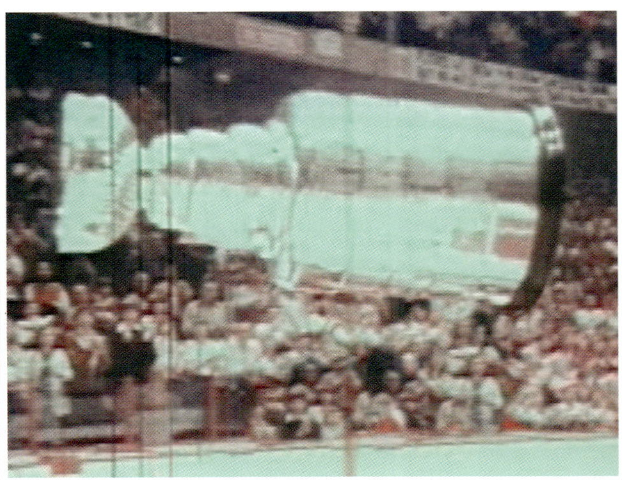
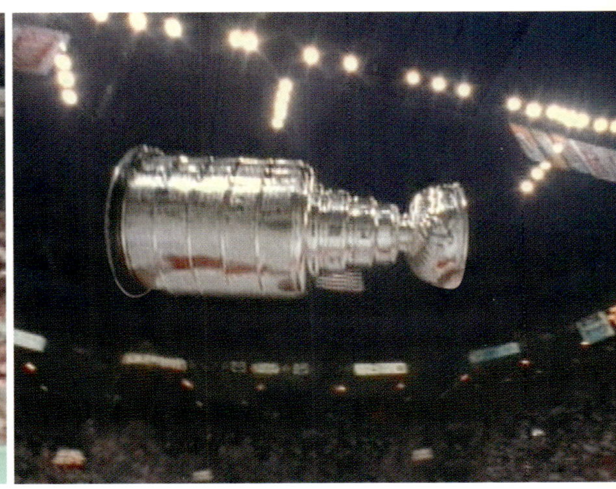

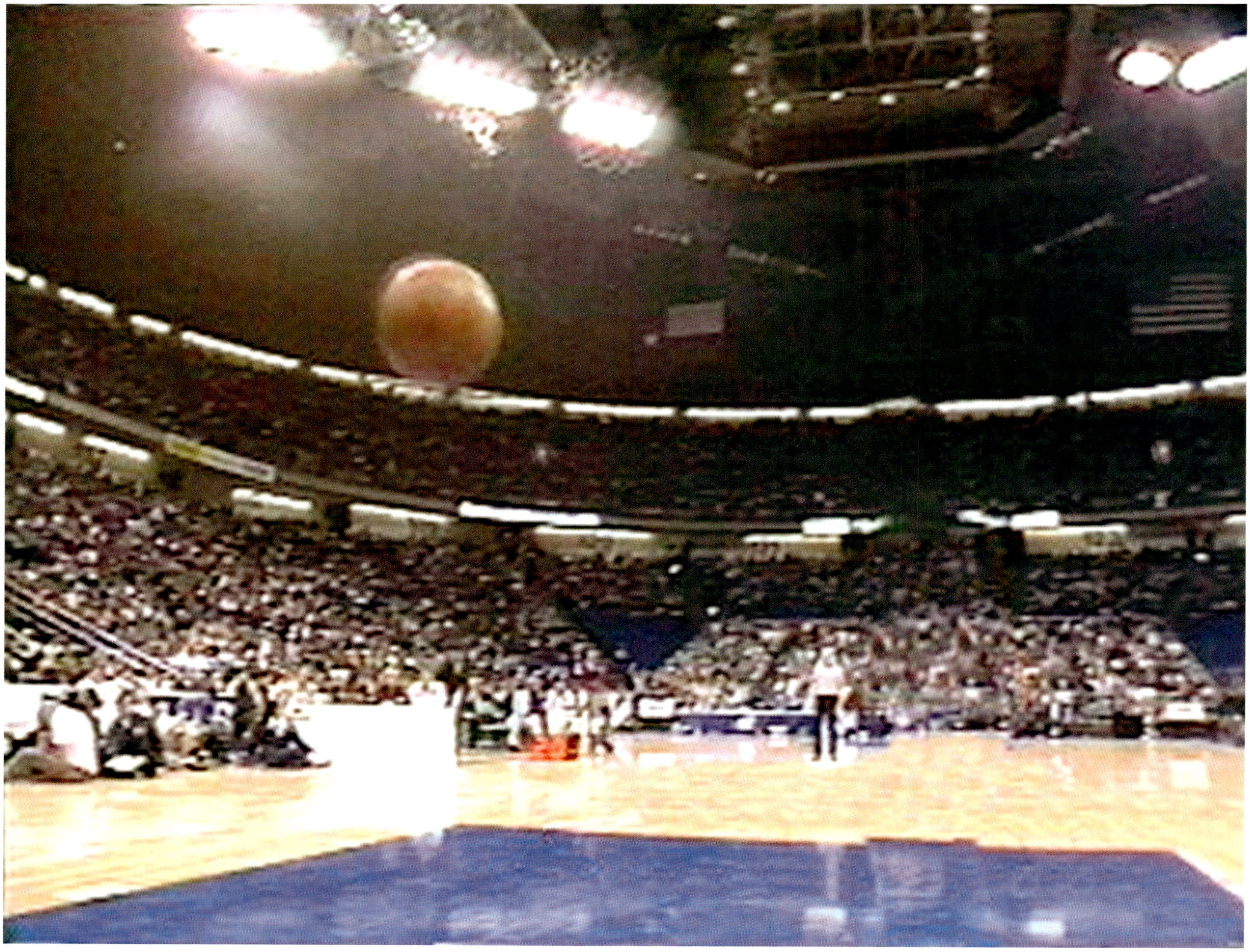

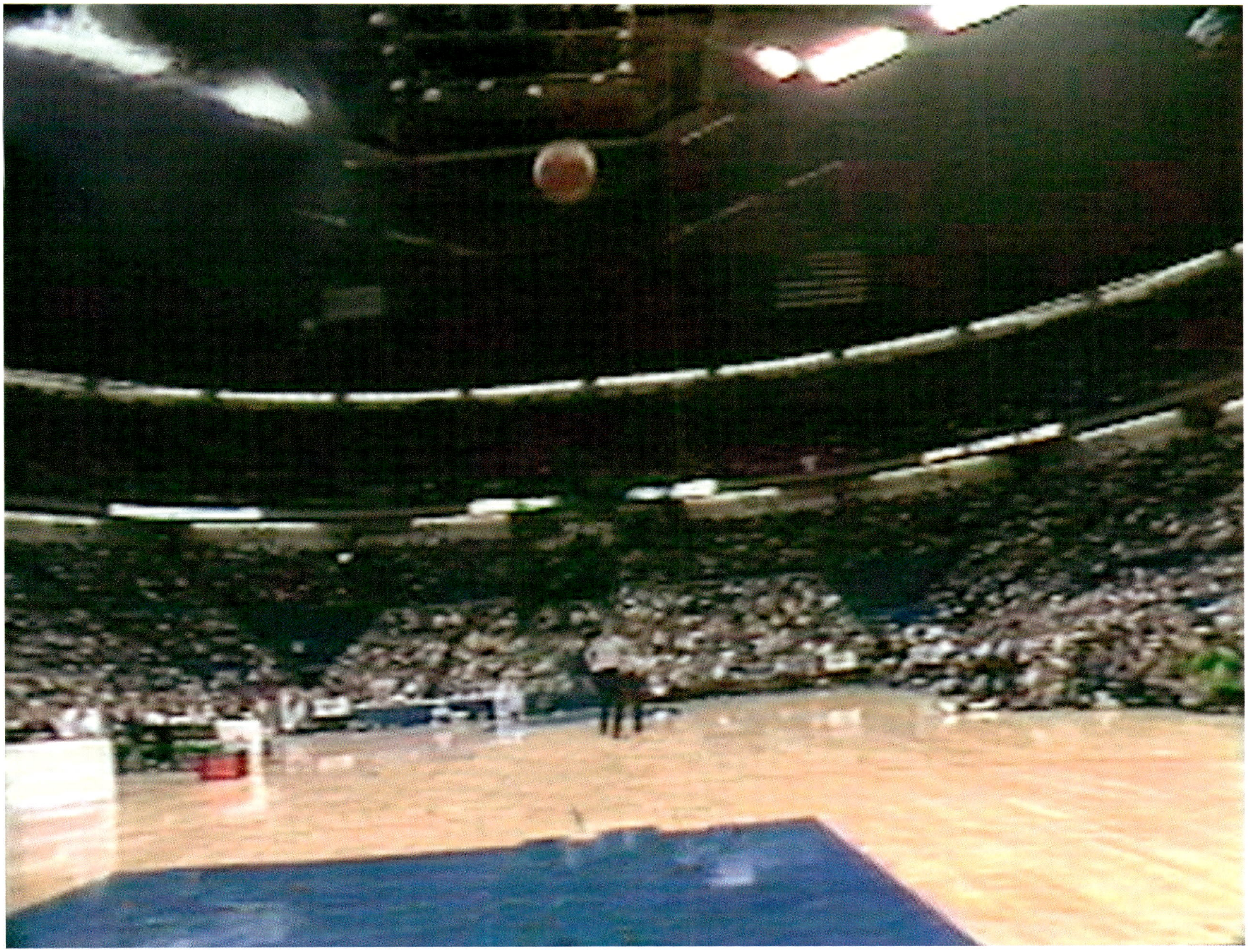

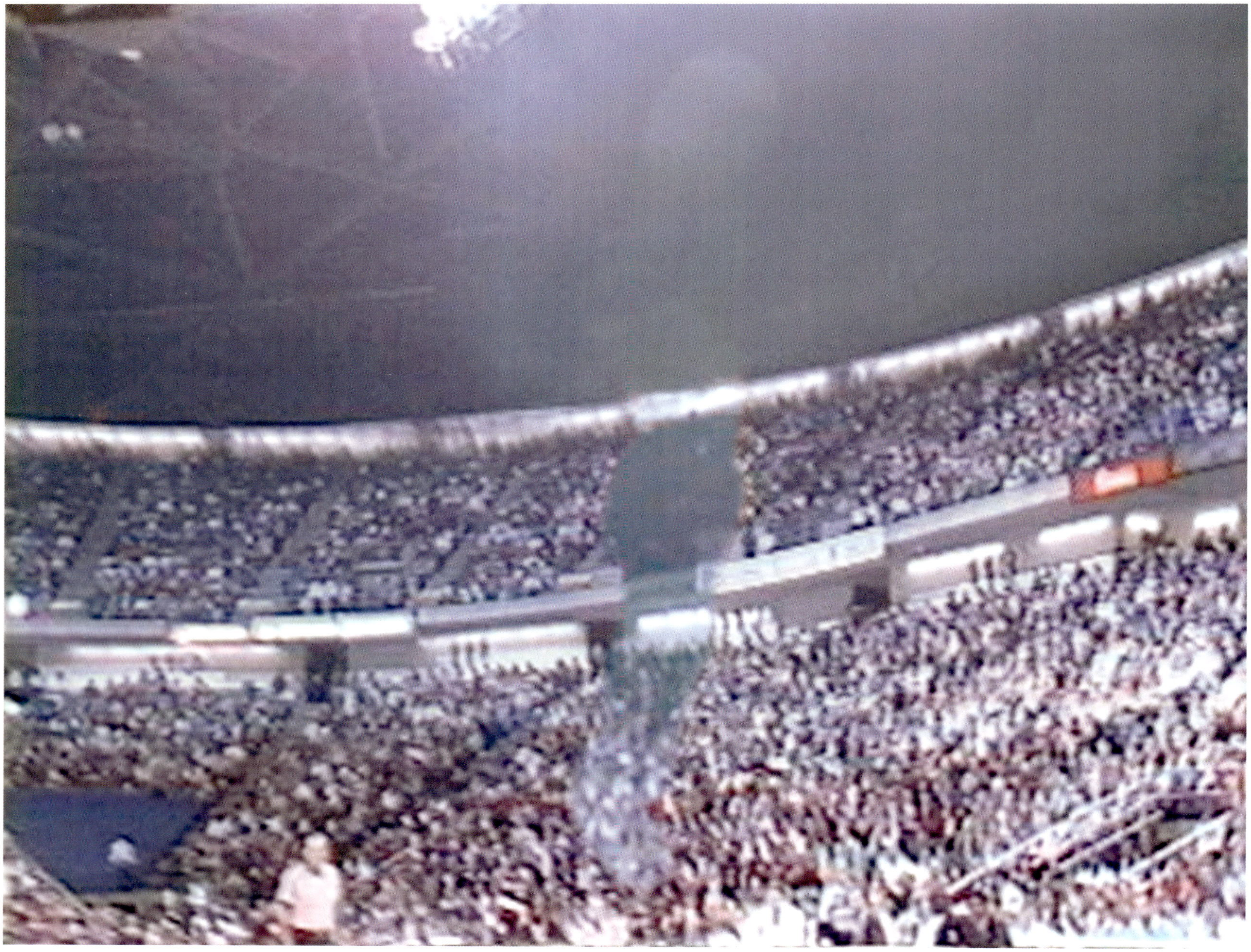

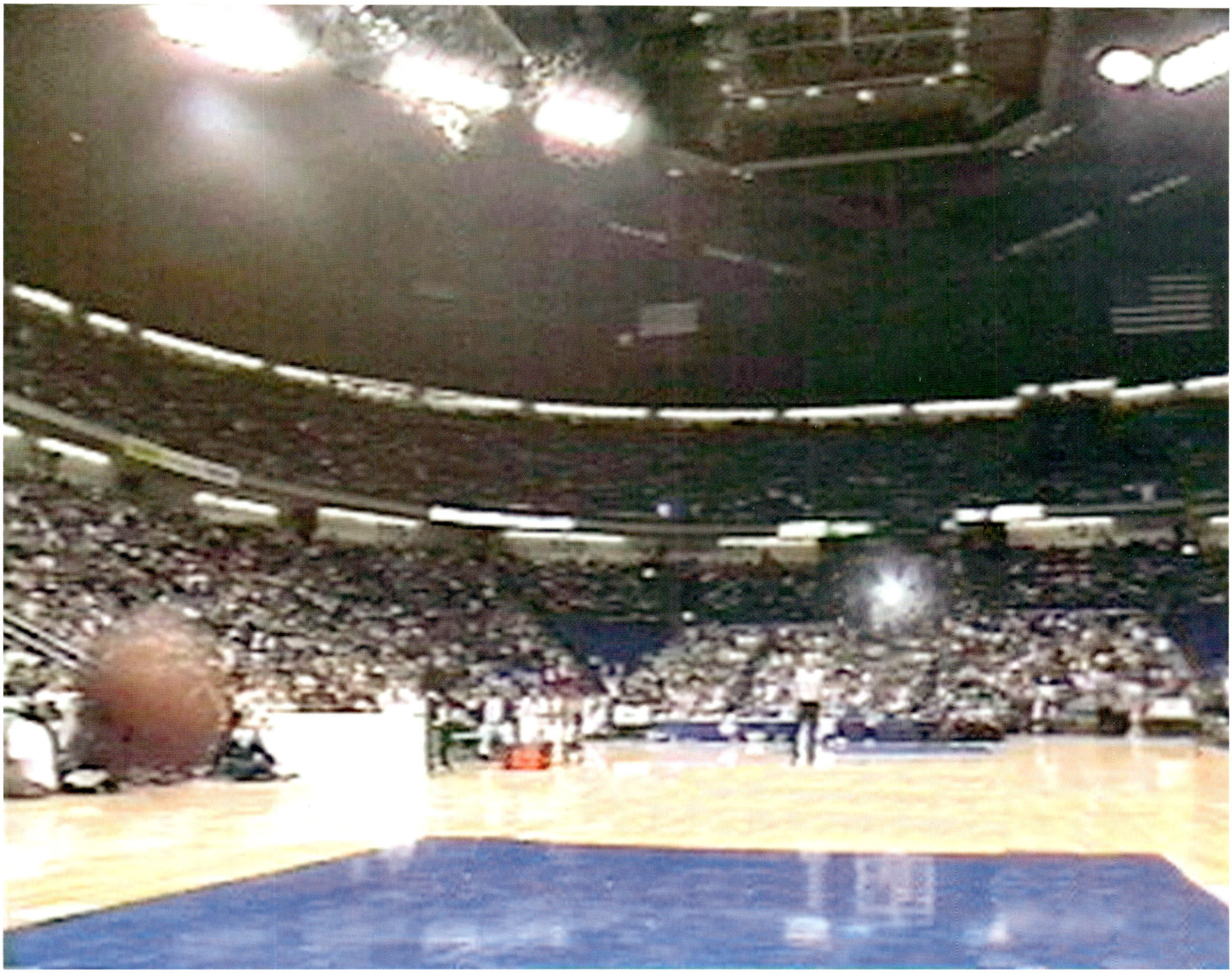

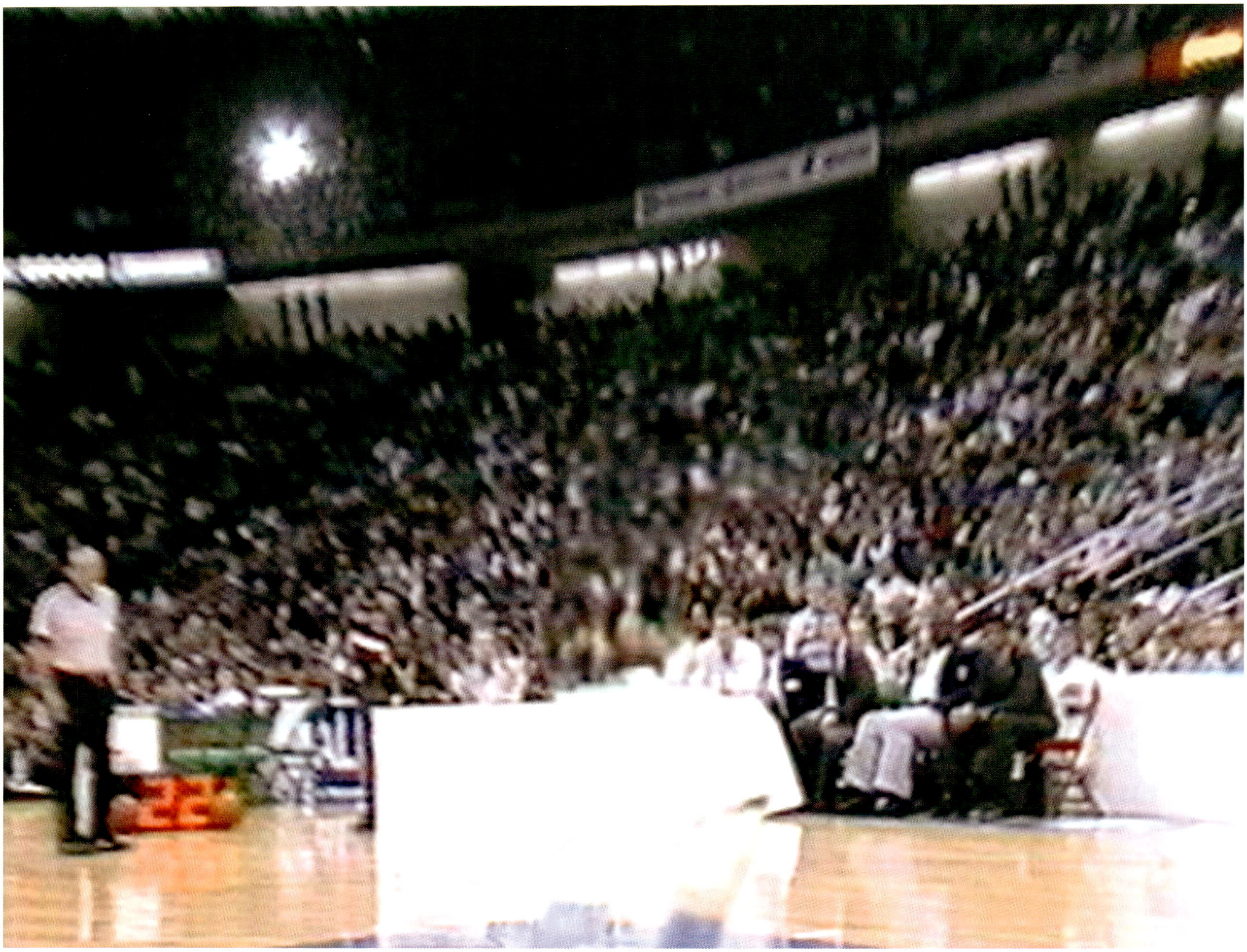

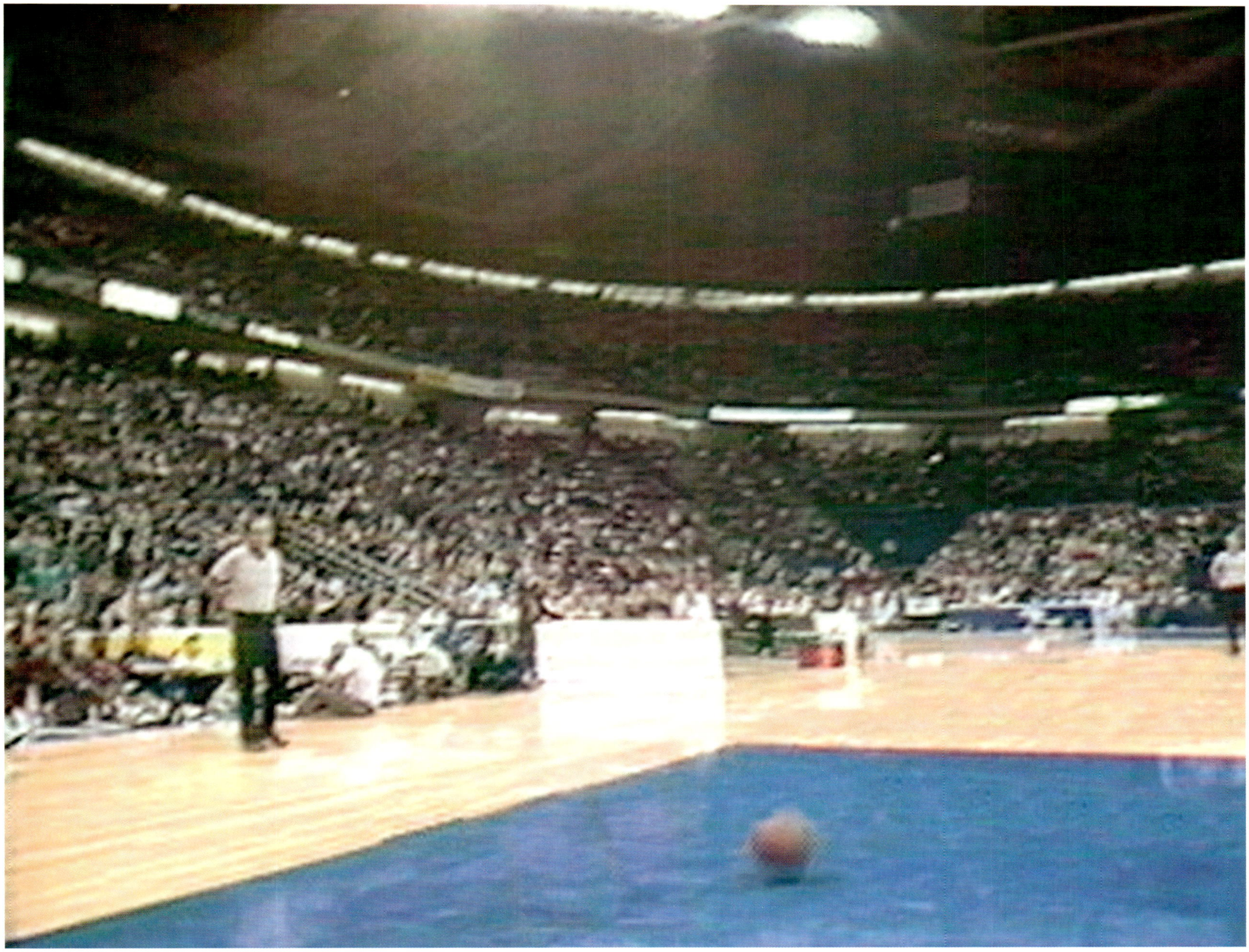

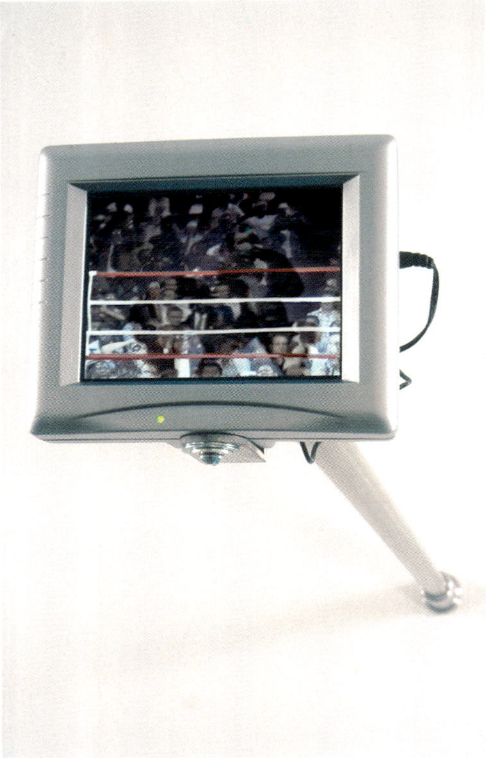

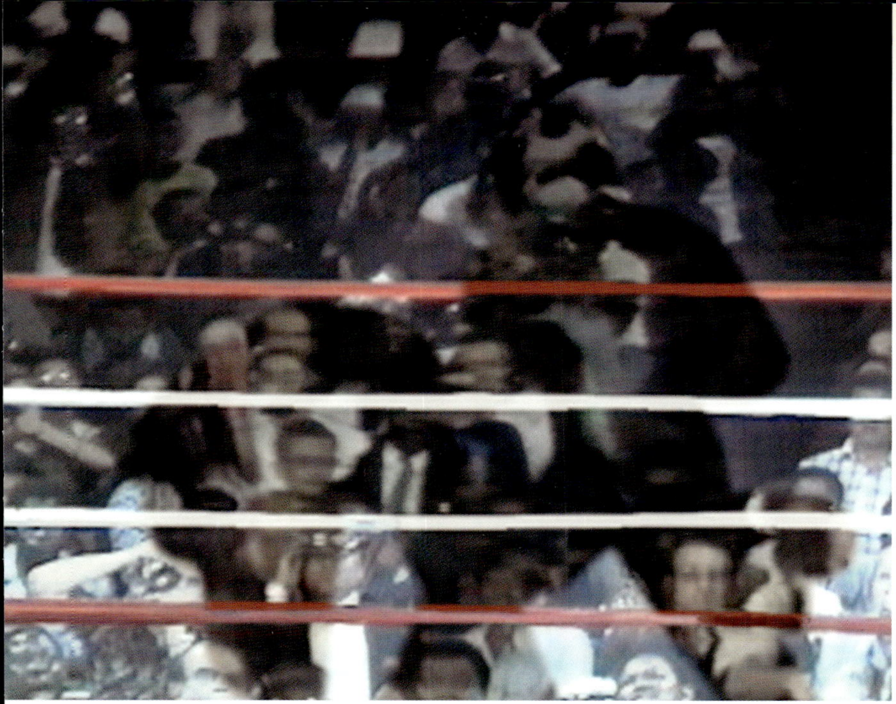

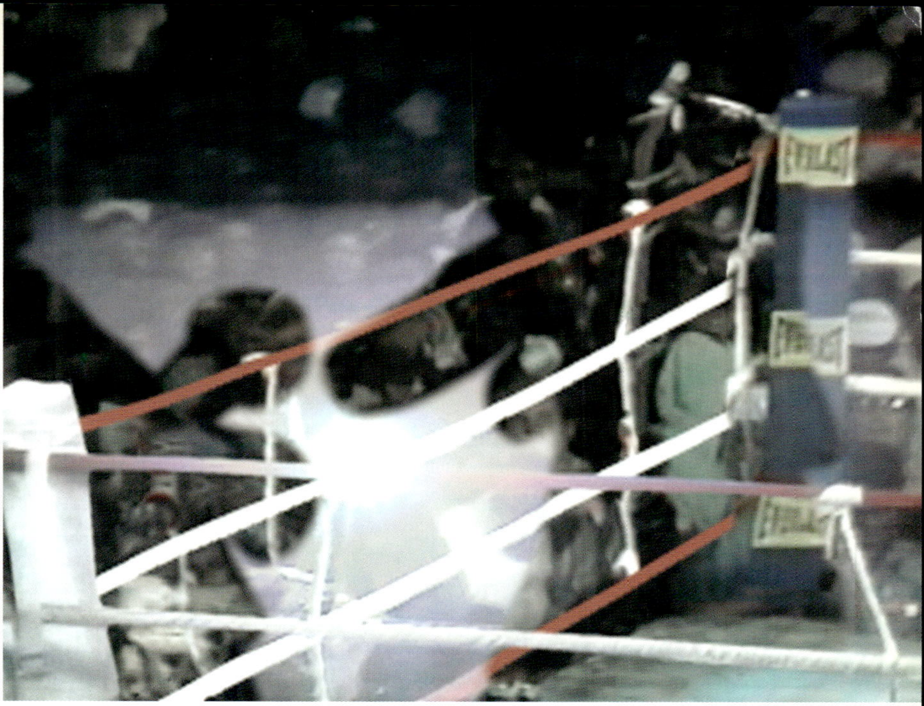
EVERLAST

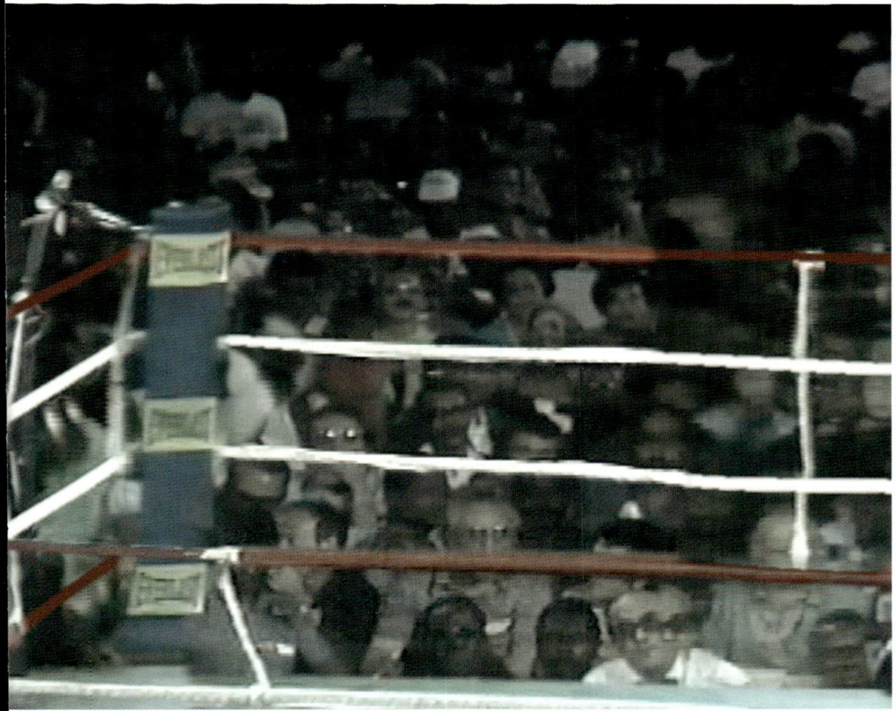
EVERLAST

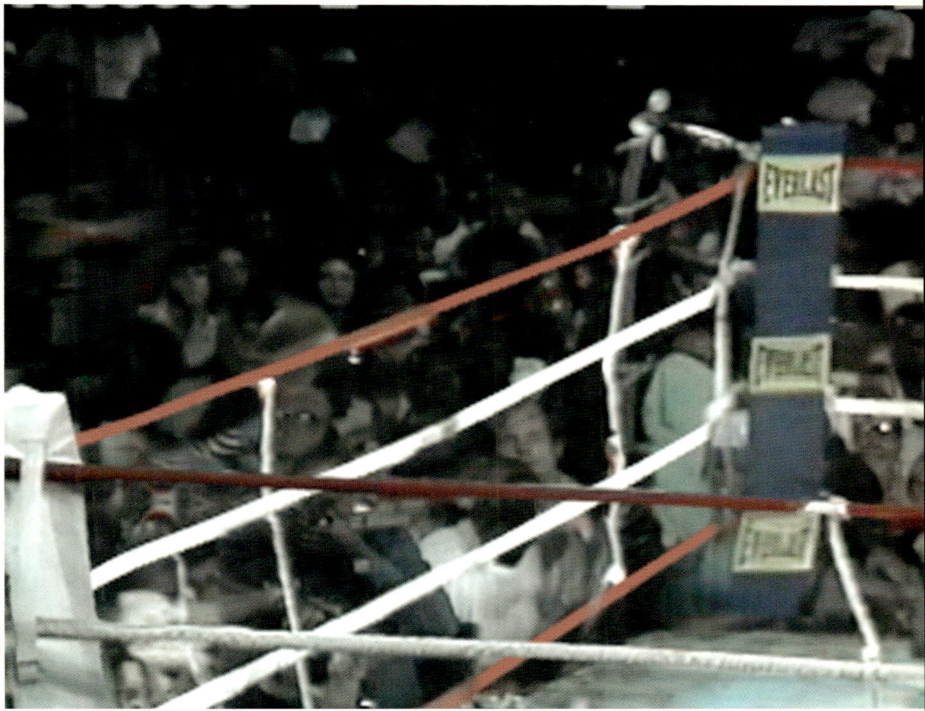
EVERLAST

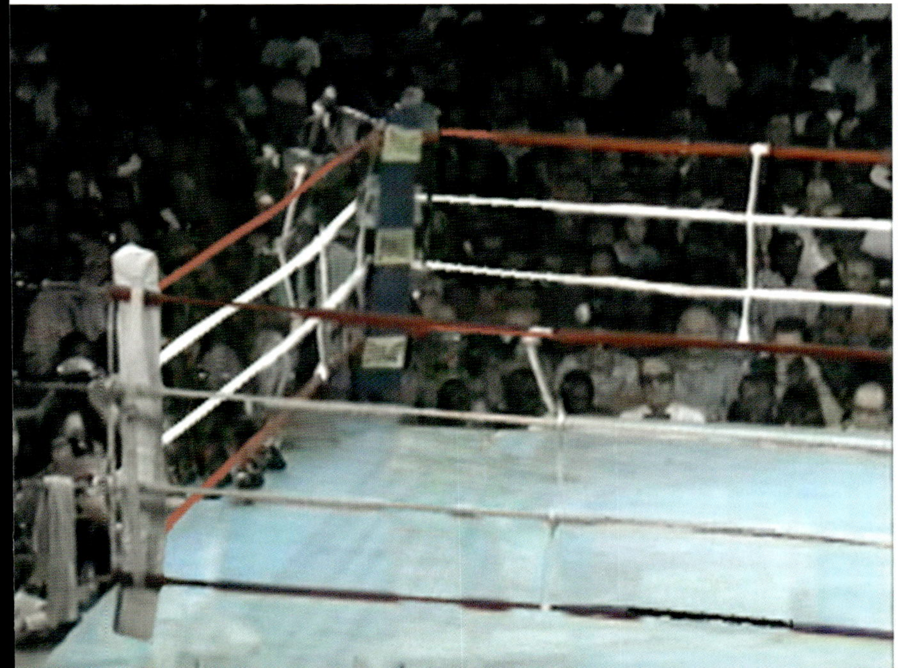

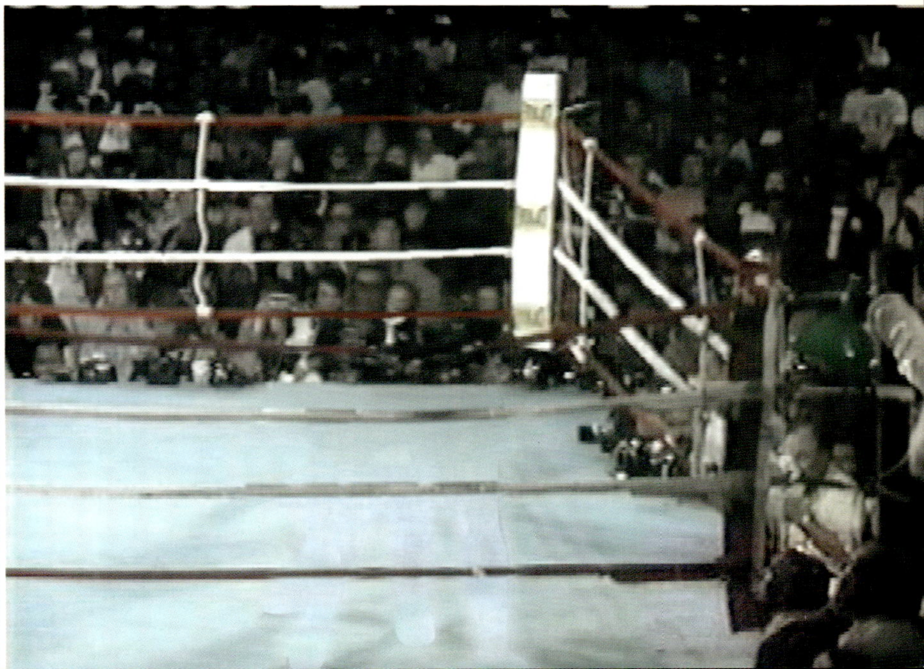

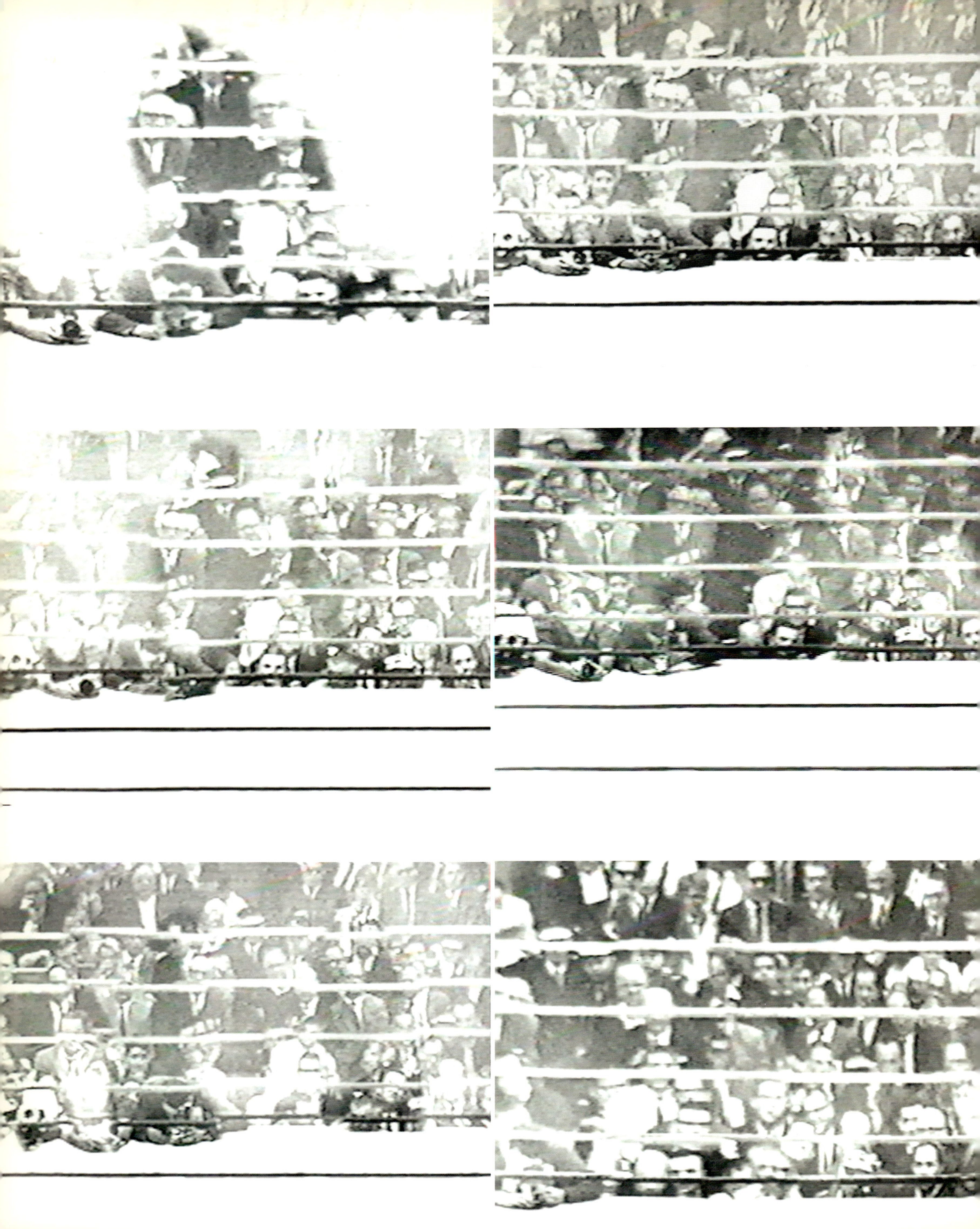

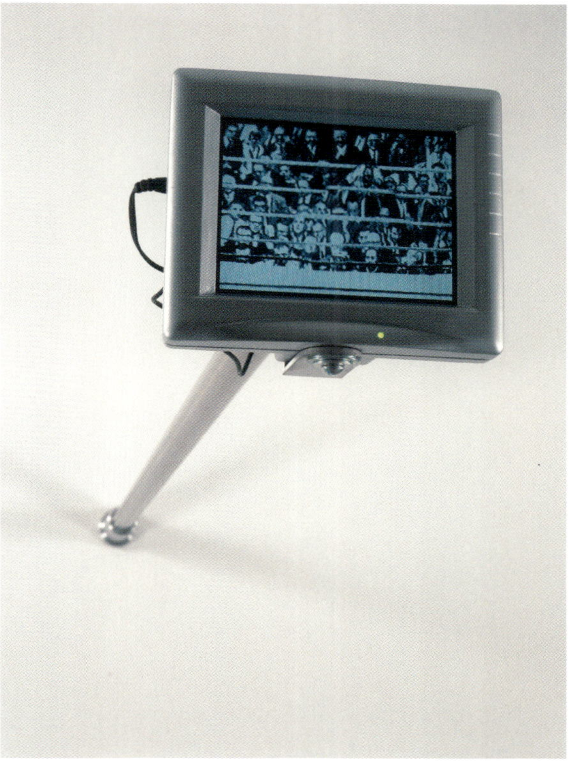

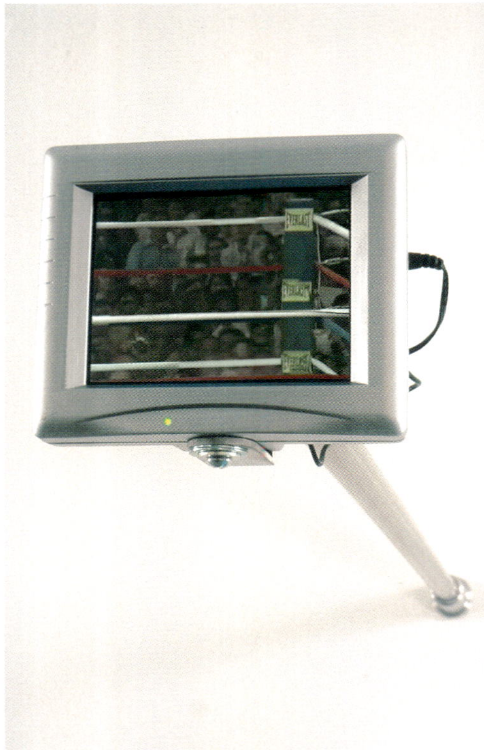

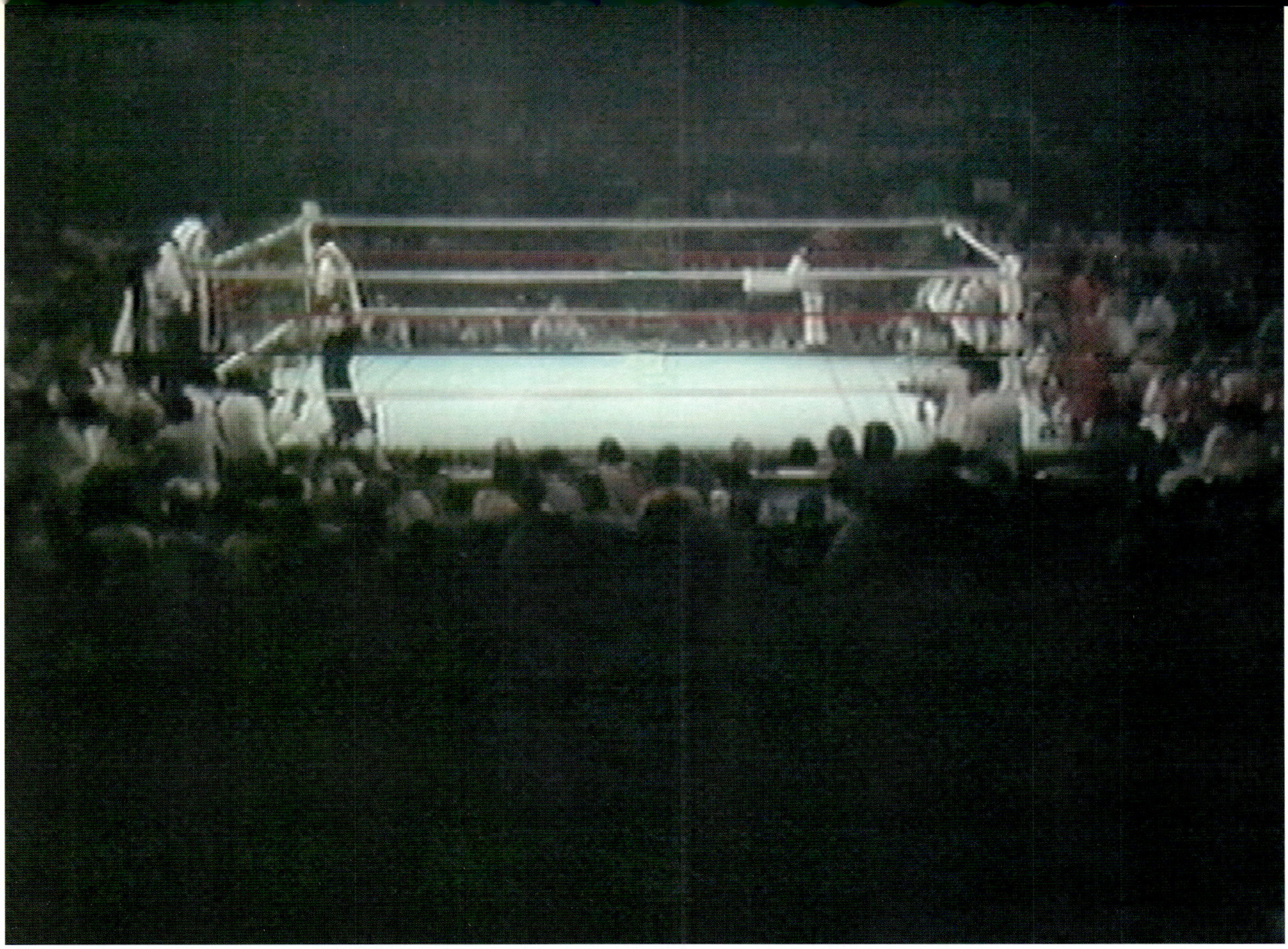

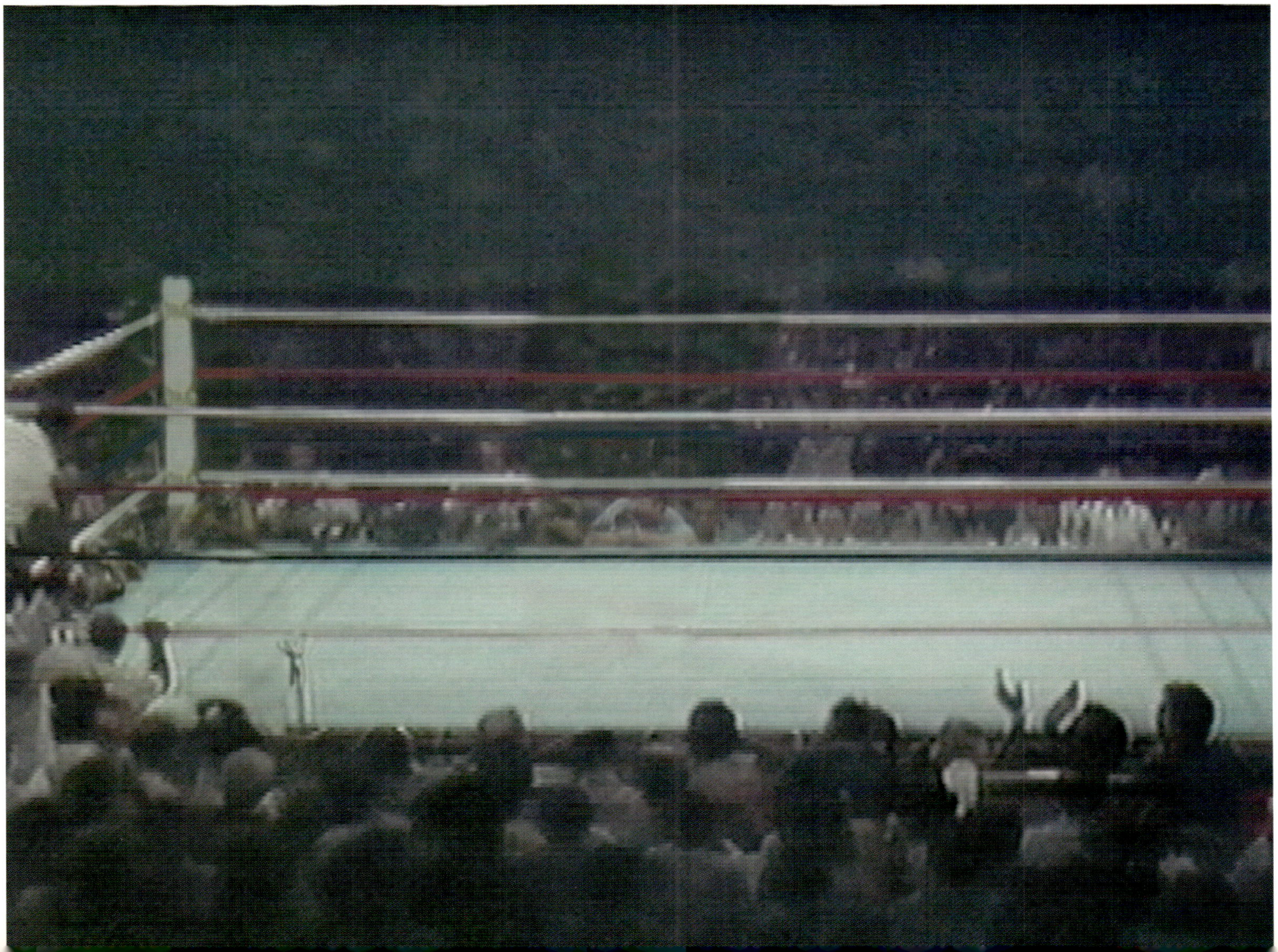

DUTCH INTERIOR

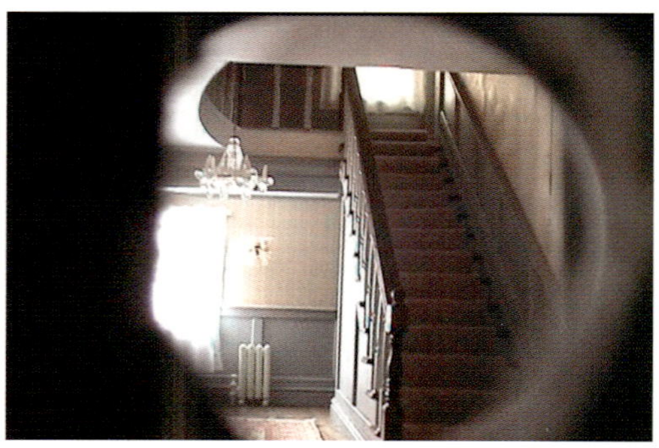

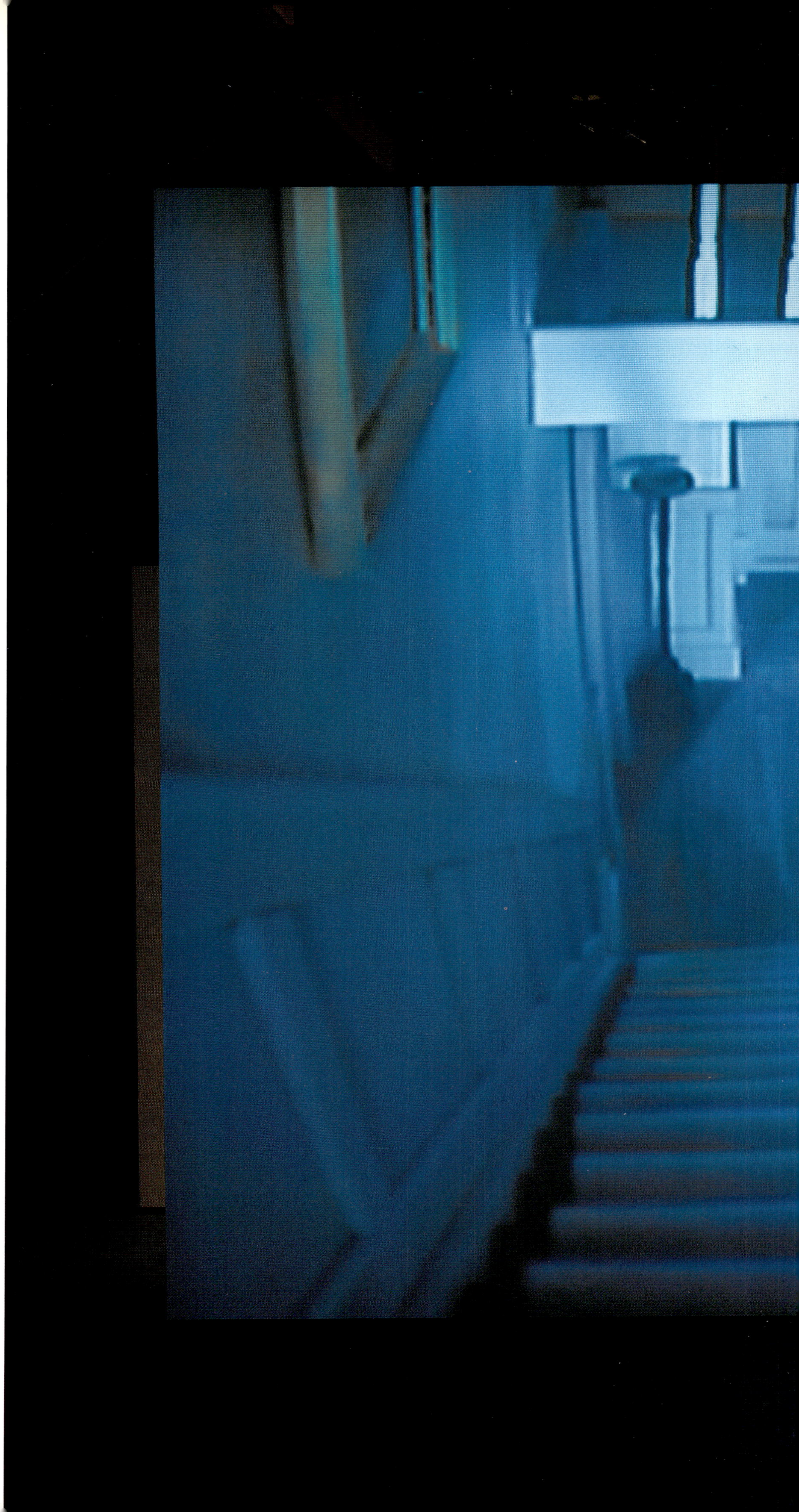

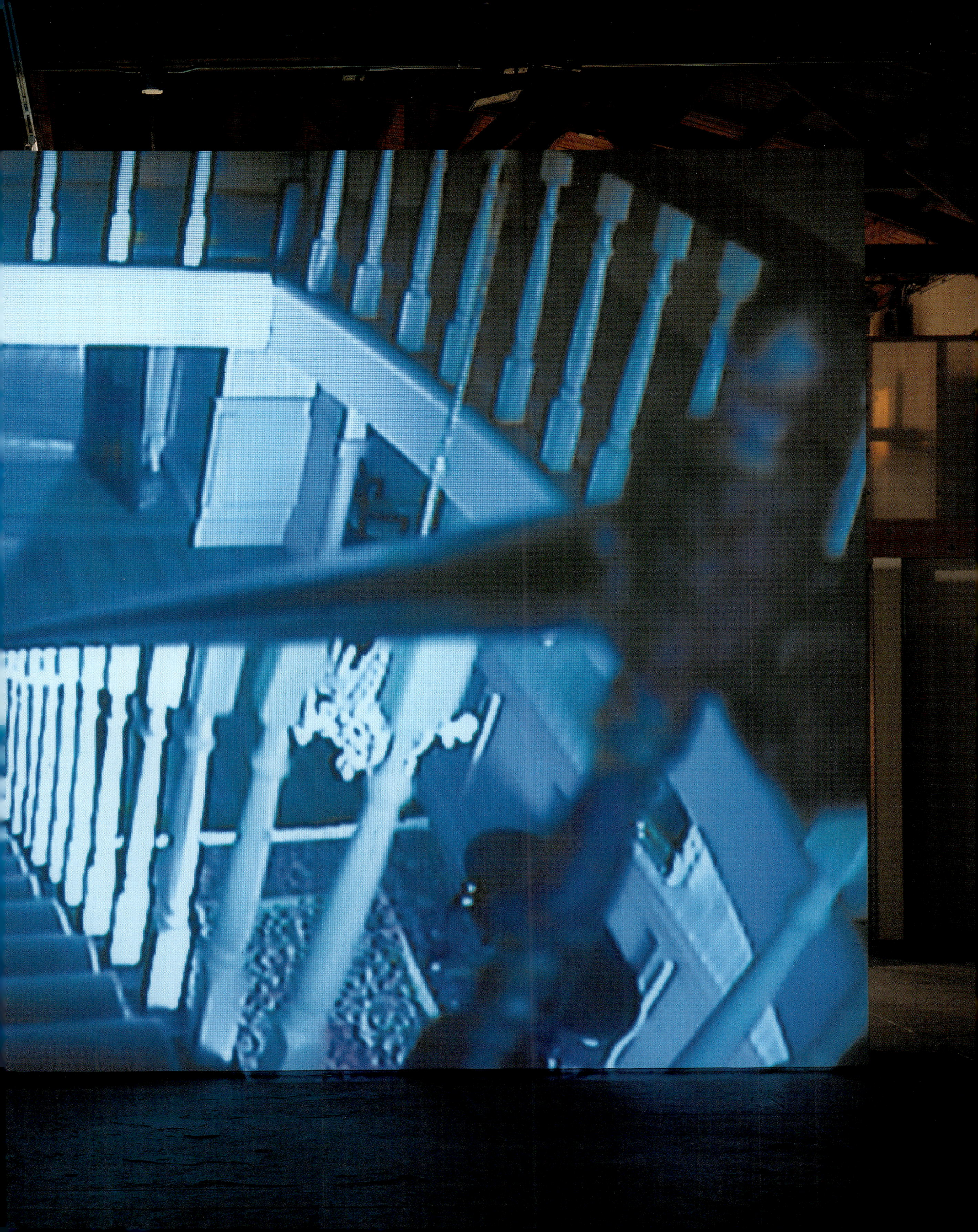

SELF-PORTRAIT AS A FOUNTAIN 2000

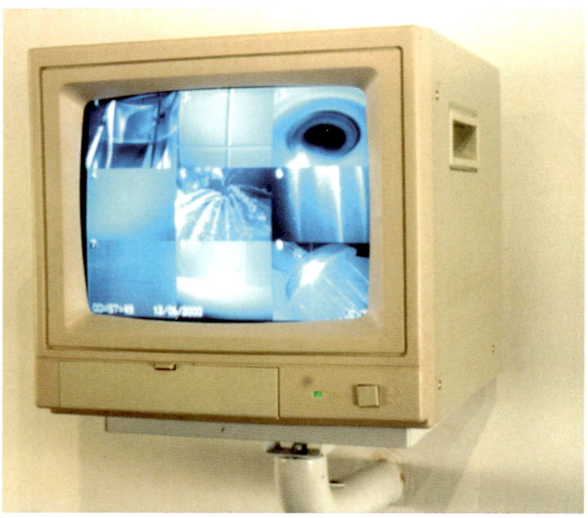

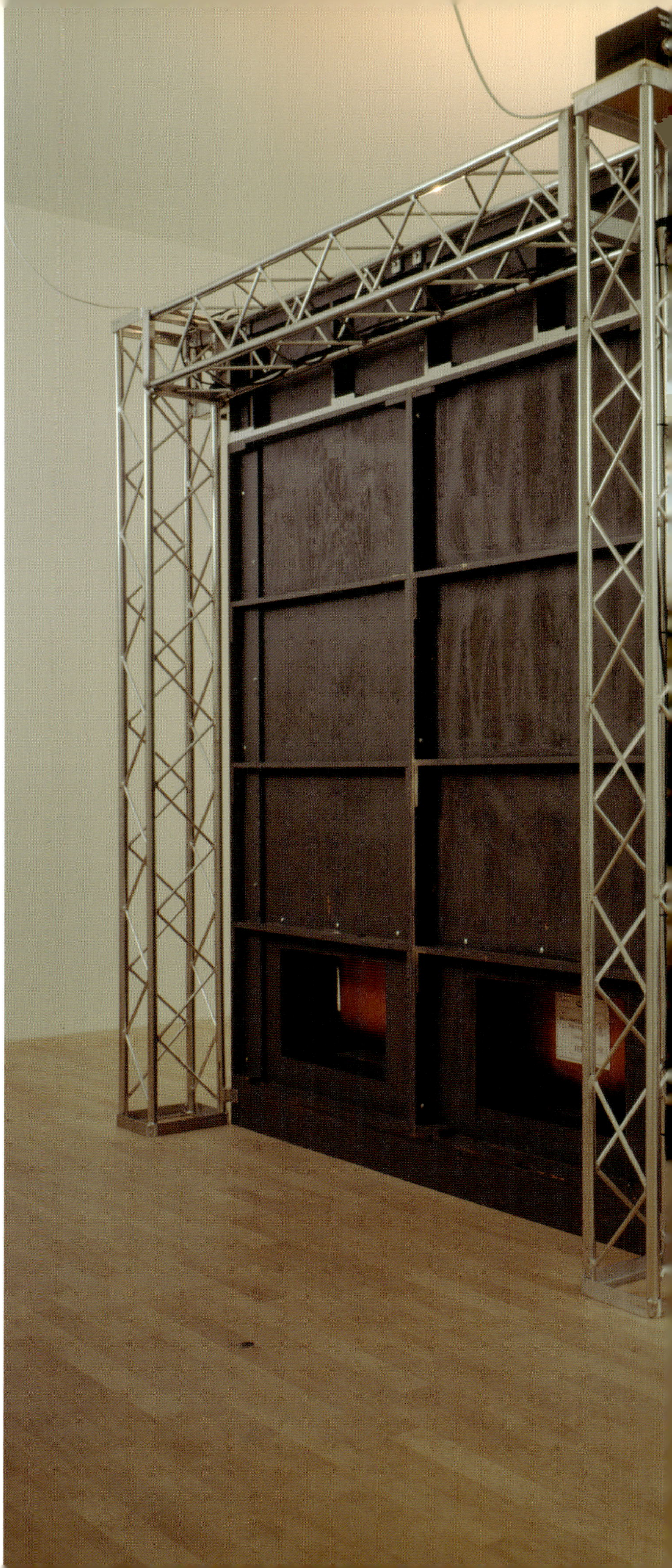

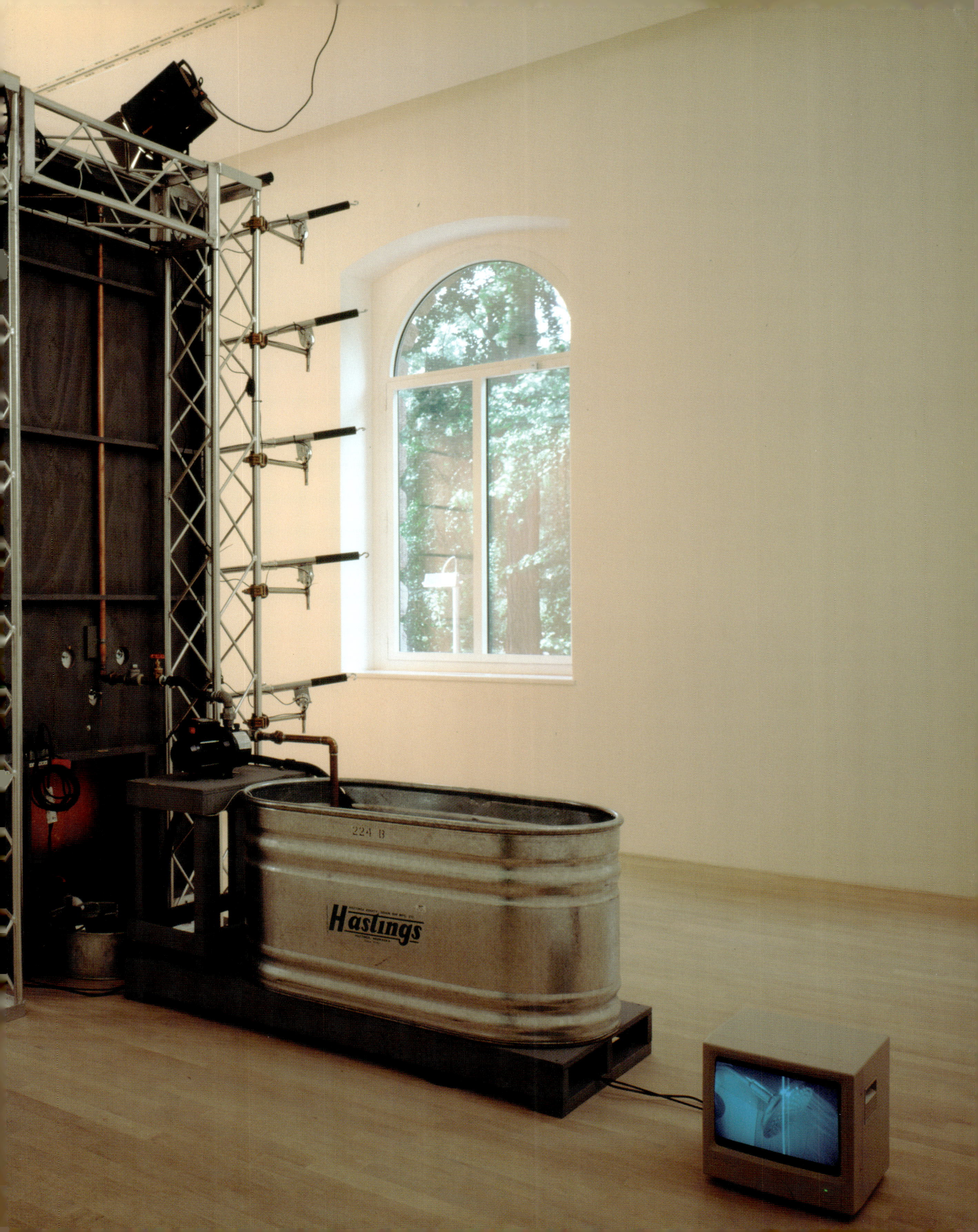
224 B
Hastings

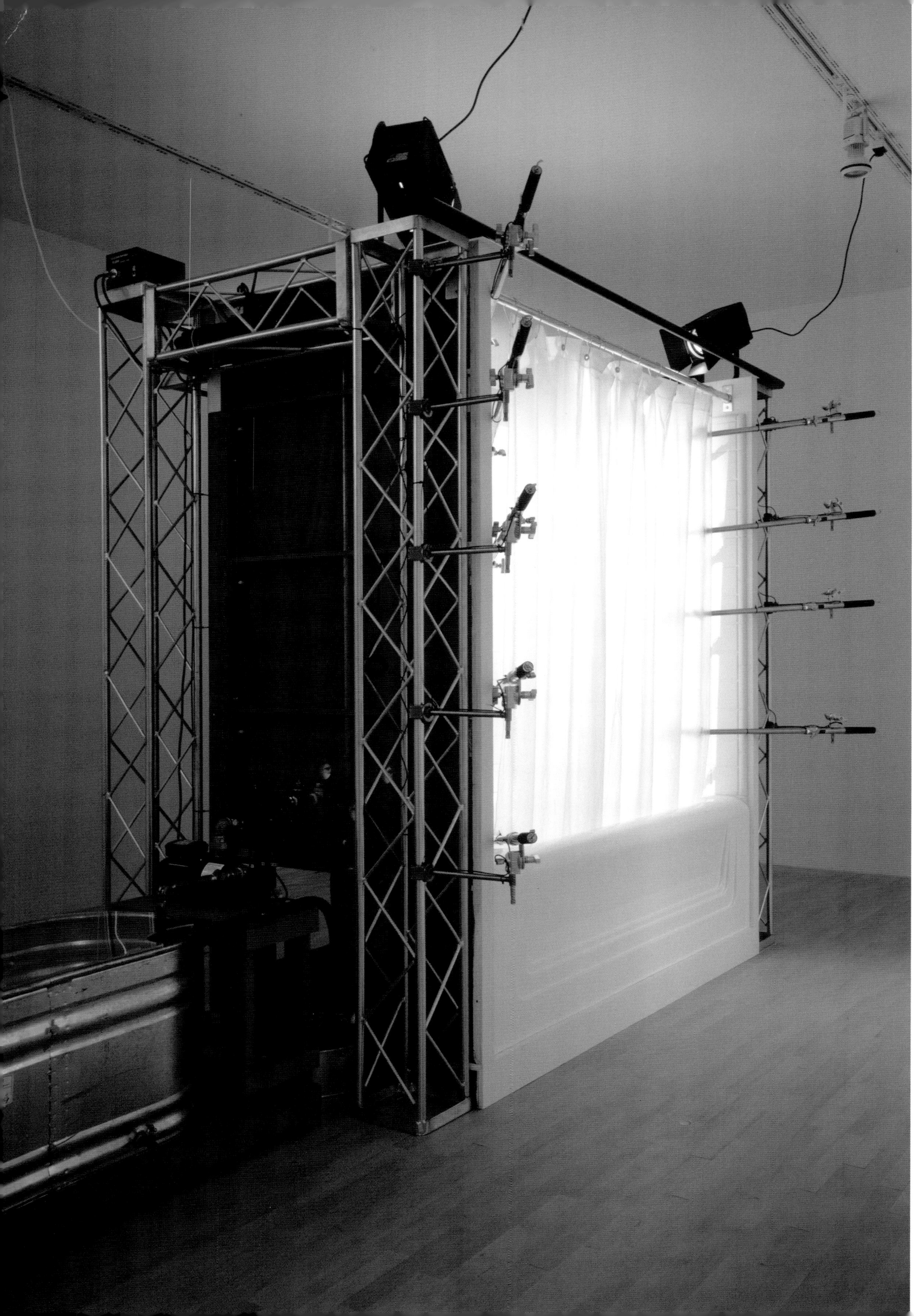

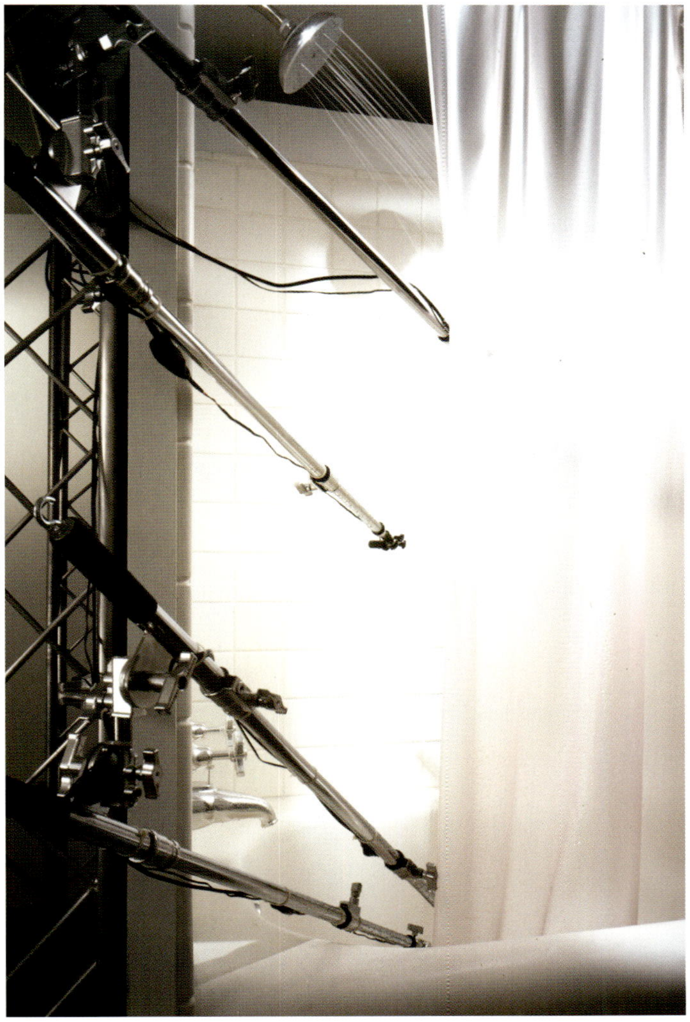

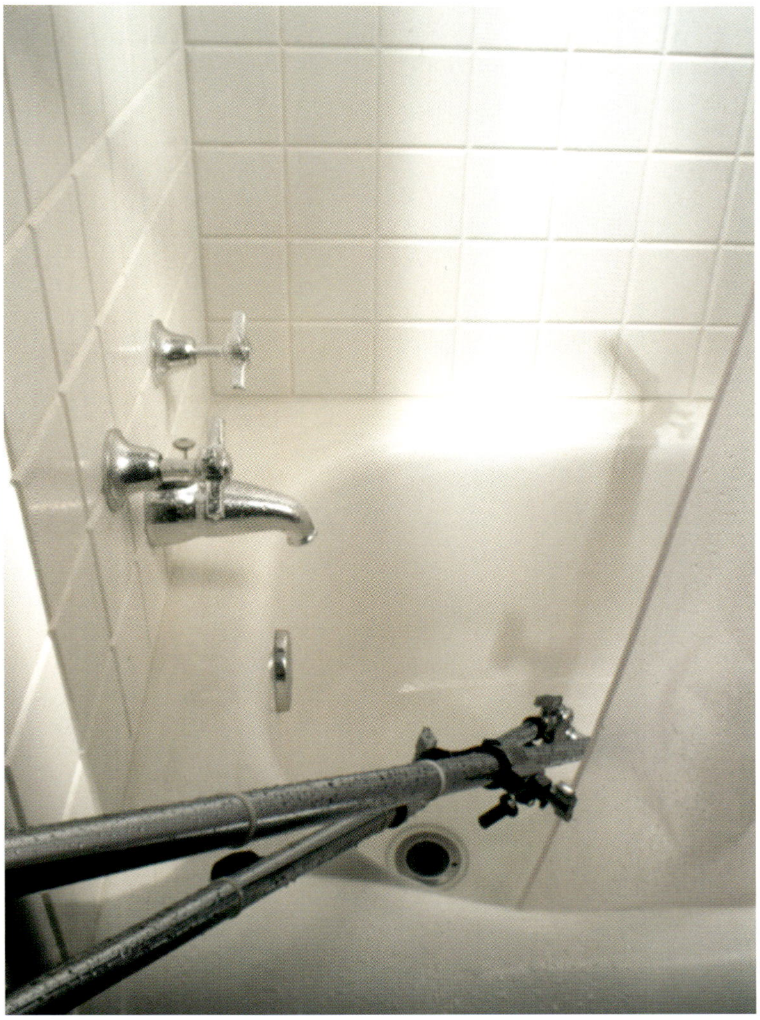

PAUL PFEIFFER AND THOMAS RUFF IN CONVERSATION

PAUL PFEIFFER UND THOMAS RUFF IM GESPRÄCH

PP: Bei der Vorbereitung auf dieses Gespräch bin ich auf eine Bemerkung von dir gestoßen, derzufolge du eher mit dem Geist siehst als mit dem Auge. Das entspricht sehr stark meiner eigenen Auffassung davon, worum es beim Kunstmachen geht.

TR: Ich habe diese Aussage im Hinblick auf die Serie stereoskopischer Bilder gemacht. Bei der Arbeit an ihnen habe ich festgestellt, dass nicht das Auge, sondern das Gehirn die aktivste Rolle bei der Wahrnehmung spielt. Wenn man sich ein Paar stereoskopischer Bilder ansieht, erscheinen sie zweidimensional. Doch wenn man sie auf angemessene Weise, das heißt mit einem Stereoskop betrachtet, dann werden die beiden flachen Bilder dreidimensional. Die Wahrnehmungsfrage stellt sich nicht nur bei stereoskopischen Bildern, sondern bei Kunstwerken in allen Medien. Betrachtet man ein Gemälde ohne das Gehirn, dann besteht es nur aus Ölklumpen auf einer Leinwand. Doch die ganze Bedeutung beziehungsweise der Rest des Kunstwerks erschließt sich erst, wenn man von seinem Gehirn Gebrauch macht.

PP: Für mich beschreibt dies auch die Arbeit des Künstlers. Mit einem Medium umgehen lernen bedeutet mehr als nur die Koordination eines scharfen Auges und einer ruhigen Hand. Es geht dabei darum, ein tieferes Verständnis für die eigene Beziehung zu diesem Medium zu entwickeln. Ich habe neulich darüber nachgedacht, dass Digitalvideo und -Fotografie eine visuelle Sprache darstellen, die nie für das spezifische künstlerische Projekt gedacht war, mit dem ich mich befasse. Meines Erachtens wurden die Instrumente der digitalen Bilderzeugung zunächst für militärische Zwecke entwickelt und dann von der Unterhaltungs- und Werbeindustrie übernommen und verfeinert. Für mich handelt es sich dabei um eine geborgte Sprache. Die Verwendung dieser Instrumente im Rahmen der Kunstproduktion scheint immer mit dem Problem einherzugehen, dass man sich mit etwas herumschlägt, das nicht ganz genau passt, weil es für einen völlig anderen Zweck entworfen wurde.

TR: Natürlich wurden die Fotografie und andere neue oder neuere Medien – Film, Video und so weiter – aus anderen Gründen erfunden, als um damit Kunst zu machen. Zugleich meine ich aber, dass man Bilder schon immer benutzt hat, um alle möglichen unterschiedlichen Informationen bereitzustellen. Bilder werden aus investigativen, politischen oder persönlichen Gründen gemacht. Menschen haben seit Jahrtausenden Bilder gemacht und sie sich angesehen. Die Funktion und das Verständnis der Bilder ist einem ständigen Wandel unterworfen. In der Welt der Bildproduktion lässt sich das gut verfolgen: In einem bestimmten Kontext wird ein neues Werkzeug erfunden, dann wird es für einen völlig anderen Gebrauch weiterentwickelt und schließlich von allen möglichen Interessen angewandt. Und natürlich werden diese Instrumente später auch zur Herstellung von Kunst benutzt.

PP: While preparing for this conversation I came across a statement you made about seeing with the mind rather then seeing with the eye. This resonates strongly with my own sense of what art making is about.

TR: The statement was made in regard to the series of stereoscopic images. Working on them I realized it is not the eye but the brain that plays the most active part in perception. If you look at a pair of stereoscopic images they appear two-dimensional. But if you look at them in a proper way or with a stereoscopic apparatus, the two flat images become three-dimensional. The question of perception does not occur only with stereoscopic images but with artwork in all media. If you look at a painting without your brain, it's just clumps of oil on a canvas. All the meaning or the rest of the artwork comes by using your brain.

PP: For me this also describes the labor of the artist. Learning to use a medium is more than a technical matter, more than the coordination of a sharp eye and a steady hand. It's about gaining a deeper understanding of your relationship to the medium. I've been thinking lately about how digital video and photography represent a visual language never intended for the particular art-making project I'm involved in. As I see it, digital imaging tools were first developed for military use, then adopted and refined by the entertainment and advertising industries. So for me they're a borrowed language. Using these tools to make art seems always a problem of wrestling with something that doesn't quite fit properly because it was designed for a totally different purpose.

TR: Photography and other new or newer media – film, video and so on – were of course invented for other reasons than for producing art. At the same time I think images have always been used to provide all kinds of different information: images are made for investigational reasons, political or personal reasons. People have been making and looking at images for thousands of years. There has always been a constant shifting of the function and understanding of images. You can see this happening in the world of visual production: a new tool is invented in one context, then developed for a completely different use, then taken over by all kinds of other interests. And of course those tools are also later used to produce art.

PP: There's certainly a constant exchange going on between people working in different fields or different industries. Still, I think there is a distinction to be made between art making and mass media programming, which is still by far the predominant use of video today. Artists are engaged in a more focused kind of inquiry. I see this in your work: it's like a scientific investigation. I say that because there's a real rigorousness about the way that you give form to your work. Words like detachment and neutrality struck me as I was reading about your work; there was this idea of photography as capturing only the surface. In relation to the *Portraits* one thing I found interesting was the idea of avoiding or attempting to

PP: Mit Sicherheit gibt es einen ständigen Austausch zwischen Menschen, die auf verschiedenen Gebieten oder in verschiedenen Industrien arbeiten. Dennoch meine ich, dass man zwischen der Herstellung von Kunst und der Programmierung durch die Massenmedien unterscheiden muss, denn dort wird Video auch heute noch bei weitem am häufigsten eingesetzt. Künstler gehen wesentlich konzentrierter damit um. Ich sehe das an deinem Werk, das einer wissenschaftlichen Untersuchung ähnelt. Ich sage das, weil die Art, wie du deinem Werk Gestalt verleihst, etwas sehr Strenges hat. Als ich Texte über dein Werk las, fielen mir Worte wie Distanz und Neutralität besonders auf; es gibt da diese Idee, dass die Fotografie nur die Oberfläche festhält. Im Hinblick auf die *Porträts* fand ich die Idee besonders interessant, eine psychologische Deutung zu vermeiden oder zumindest zu versuchen, sie zu vermeiden, das Beharren darauf, keine Empfindungen zu zeigen. Dabei denke ich an den Charakter einer leidenschaftslosen Untersuchung, bei der man sich nicht selbst betrachtet, sondern versucht, sie zu umgehen, um zu einer tieferen Wahrheit zu gelangen. Gleichzeitig sehe ich einen Widerspruch in deinem Werk, da so viele der von dir verwendeten Motive mit Bedeutung aufgeladen sind. Es hat den Anschein, als hättest du gerade solche Bilder gewählt, die am meisten zu einer psychologischen Deutung einladen oder die den Wunsch des Betrachters nach einer Erklärung oder irgendeiner Art narrativer Schließung steigern. Für mich ist das ein sehr interessanter Widerspruch. Du forderst die Betrachter auf, mit dir zusammen einen Schritt zurückzutreten und die Welt leidenschaftslos zu betrachten, und zugleich verführst du die Betrachter und bringst sie in eine Position, in der sie am anfälligsten für ihre eigenen Empfindungen und persönlichen Erfahrungen sind.

TR: Als ich über die *Porträts* nachdachte, entschloss ich mich, zu dem wesentlichen Bild zurückzukehren. Was ist ein Porträt? Wahrscheinlich hatte es etwas mit meiner persönlichen Erfahrung zu tun; ich dachte, das perfekte Porträt sei ein Passbild. Daher versuchte ich, diese Art Fotografie nachzuahmen. Es gab verschiedene Gründe, warum mir diese Fotografien ideal zu sein schienen. Vor allem werden Passfotos zusammen mit all den übrigen Informationen, die in einem Pass aufgelistet sind, verwendet, um einen Menschen zu identifizieren. Das Bildnis selbst zeigt nur die sichtbare Oberfläche einer Person. Wenn man nur diese Oberfläche nimmt und alle anderen Informationen tilgt, wie ich das getan habe, indem ich nur das Passfoto benutzte und nicht den Namen, das Alter, die Adresse usw., dann blickt man einfach nur in das Gesicht eines Menschen. Mir ging es darum, die Persönlichkeit des Porträtierten einzufangen, auch wenn ich nicht glaube, dass man die ganze Persönlichkeit eines Menschen in einer einzigen Fotografie erfassen kann. Man braucht eine Million

avoid psychological interpretation in the portrait, an insistence on no showing of feeling. This makes me think of the nature of a dispassionate investigation, where you are not looking at yourself but trying to get beyond you to see a greater truth. At the same time I see a contradiction in your work in that so much of the imagery you use is loaded. It seems that you are specifically choosing images that are the most inviting of psychological interpretation, or that heighten the viewer's desire for an explanation, or for some kind of narrative closure. It's a very interesting contradiction to me. You are asking the viewer to step back with you and to look at the world dispassionately and at the same time you are also seducing the viewer into a position where they are the most vulnerable to their own emotions and personal experiences.

TR: When I thought about the *Portraits* I decided I had to go back to the very essential image. What is a portrait? Probably it had to do with my personal experience; I thought the perfect portrait is a passport photograph. So I tried to imitate this type of photograph. There were different reasons why I believed that those photographs were ideal. First of all passport photographs are used to identify a person together with all the information that is listed in your passport. The portrait itself shows only the visible surface of the person. If you take only this surface and erase all the other information, as I did by using just the passport image and not the name, age, address and so on, you are looking at just the face of a human being. I was interested in capturing the personality of the sitter even though I do not believe that one can capture the whole personality of a human being with only one photograph. You need a million photographs to explain all the different facets of a person. But my aim was to take only one very precise photograph of a person. A single photograph can only show the surface, it can't go beyond the skin of a person. I was trying to get rid of all the false traces that are connected with portraits and later on with architectural photographs or newspaper photographs or scientific photographs. I wanted to go back to the very basic image.

I photographed my friends at the art academy, as I did not know any other people in Düsseldorf at that time. The idea was to treat all of them equally, because I thought we are all equal but at the same time unique. The very straight light I used came from the idea that we do not live any more in caves using candle light, but that we live in a Western industrialized world, where bright neon light is almost everywhere.

In 1980, when I started with the *Portraits*, my friends and I had all read George Orwell's *1984* and of course we knew Big Brother and we knew that surveillance cameras were all around us. So I decided that the look into my camera should not only resemble the passport image but also show the sitter's consciousness of

Fotografien, um all die unterschiedlichen Facetten einer Person zu erklären. Doch mein Ziel war es, nur eine ganz präzise Aufnahme einer Person zu machen. Eine einzelne Aufnahme kann nur die Oberfläche zeigen, sie kann nicht unter die Haut eines Menschen dringen. Ich versuchte, all die falschen Spuren loszuwerden, die mit Porträts und später dann mit Architekturaufnahmen oder Zeitungsbildern oder wissenschaftlichen Fotografien verbunden sind. Ich wollte wieder zu dem ganz grundlegenden Bild zurückkehren.

Ich fotografierte meine Freunde in der Kunstakademie, da ich damals in Düsseldorf niemanden sonst kannte. Die Idee war, sie alle gleich zu behandeln, weil ich dachte, dass wir alle gleich seien, aber eben auch einzigartig. Das sehr direkte Licht, das ich einsetzte, beruhte auf der Einsicht, dass wir nicht mehr in Höhlen hausen und Kerzenlicht benutzen, sondern in einer westlichen industrialisierten Welt leben, in der helles Neonlicht fast allgegenwärtig ist.

1980, als ich mit den *Porträts* begann, hatten meine Freunde und ich alle Orwells *1984* gelesen, und natürlich kannten wir Big Brother und wussten, dass wir überall von Überwachungskameras umgeben waren. Daher beschloss ich, dass der Blick in die Kamera nicht einfach nur dem Passbild ähneln, sondern auch das Bewusstsein des Porträtierten für die Kamera vor ihm zeigen sollte. Ich bat den Porträtierten, selbstbewusst zu schauen, doch gleichzeitig forderte ich ihn auf, sich darüber im klaren zu sein, dass er fotografiert wird. Das Lustige für mich ist, dass der Betrachter, der sich das Bild ansieht, denkt, dass der Porträtierte ihn anschaut. Aber natürlich blickt der Porträtierte in eine Maschine, die Kamera.

PP: Das Porträt hält also nicht die Persönlichkeit des Porträtierten fest, sondern das Verhältnis des Porträtierten zur Kamera, und das Verhältnis des Betrachters zur Kamera oder dem ganzen Apparat, wenn sie sich die fertige Fotografie ansehen.

TR: Anfangs, als ich 24 x 18 cm Abzüge von den Porträts machte, verwechselten die Betrachter mitunter die Fotografie mit der Wirklichkeit. Die Leute sahen sich meine Porträts an und sagten »Das ist Petra und das ist Heinz.« Sie merkten nicht, dass sie eine Fotografie betrachteten, sondern sie betrachteten die Person. Dann beschloss ich, die Bilder in einem großen Format (210 x 160 cm) abzuziehen, damit dem Betrachter klar würde, dass er keine Person vor sich hat, sondern die Fotografie einer Person. Ich hoffte, dass es mit der Veränderung der Größe für den Betrachter offensichtlich würde, dass ein Medium zwischen der Wirklichkeit und dem Bild existiert.

Als ich deine Ausstellung im K21 sah, fragte ich mich, welche Rolle die Zeit in deinem Werk spielt. Einerseits gibt es *Orpheus Descending*, ein sehr langes Video, bei dem die Zeit konstant abläuft, und andererseits gibt es die Videoloops. Obwohl Video oder Film die

the camera in front of him. I asked the sitter to look self-confident but at the same time I asked that he be aware that he is going to be photographed. What is funny for me is that the viewer, who looks at the image, thinks that the sitter is looking at him. But of course the sitter is looking towards a machine, the camera.

PP: So the portrait does not capture the personality of the sitter, but it captures the sitter's relationship to the camera, and the viewer's relationship to the camera or to the whole apparatus, when they are looking at the finished photograph.

TR: In the beginning when I printed the portraits 24 x 18 cm, the viewer sometimes confused the photograph with reality. People were looking at my portraits and saying, »That is Petra and that is Heinz«. They did not realize that they were looking at a photograph but were looking at the person. Then I decided to print them in a large format (210 x 160 cm), so that it became obvious for the viewer that he was not looking at the person but at a photograph of the person. With the shift of size it became, I hoped, obvious to the viewer that there was a medium between the reality and the image.

When I saw your exhibition at K21 I was wondering what part time plays in your work. On the one hand you have *Orpheus Descending*, a very long video where time is passing constantly and on the other hand you have the loop videos. Even though video or film has the dimension of time, I think video loops try to avoid time. When I look, for example, at *The Pure Products Go Crazy*, even though the sequence is nearly three minutes long, it is more like a frozen image to me. It comes close to Muybridge's photographic locomotion. Repeating the loop again and again time is more or less erased. In a way it is more like a painting or like a still. There is a movement, but it is not a movement in time. It is a movement only in the two dimen-

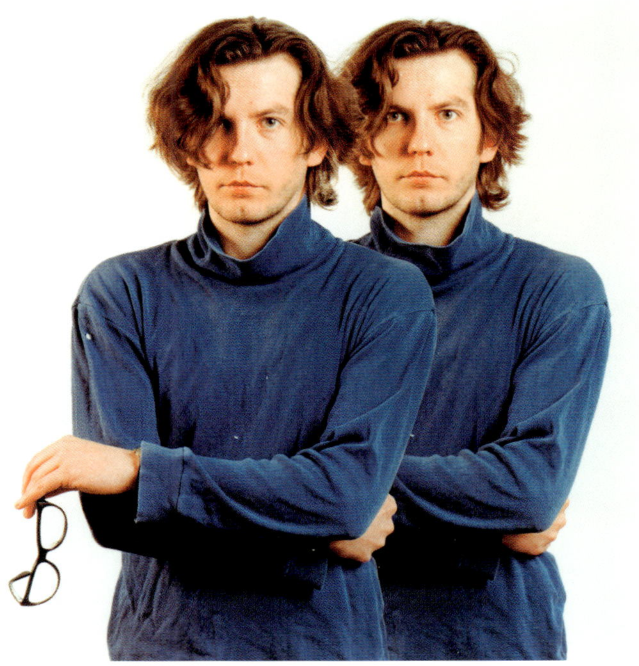

Thomas Ruff
Porträt, 1991
C-Print
185 x 190 cm

Dimension der Zeit innewohnt, denke ich, dass Videoloops versuchen, Zeit zu vermeiden. Wenn ich mir etwa *The Pure Products Go Crazy* ansehe, dann wirkt es mehr wie ein gefrorenes Bild auf mich, obwohl die Sequenz fast drei Minuten lang ist. Es kommt Muybridges fotografischer Lokomotion sehr nahe. Durch die ständige Wiederholung des Loops wird die Zeit mehr oder weniger getilgt. Irgendwie ist es eher wie ein Gemälde oder ein Standbild. Es gibt eine Bewegung, doch es ist keine Bewegung in der Zeit. Bewegung gibt es nur in den beiden Dimensionen des Bildschirms. Ich denke es handelt sich hier um ein echtes Paradox. Vielleicht funktioniert der Loop ähnlich wie die Verschlusszeit in einer Kamera. Man könnte sagen, dass selbst die Fotografie nicht gefroren ist, sondern die Zeitspanne des offenen Verschlusses repräsentiert. In den Loops verstreicht dieselbe Zeit, auch wenn es eine längere Zeit ist. Das Ganze wird mehr oder weniger zu einem Standbild.

PP: Ich bin nicht daran interessiert, Video auf narrative Weise einzusetzen, so wie man Video benutzt, um ein Melodram oder einen Dokumentarfilm zu drehen. Mir gefällt die Idee eines bewegten Bildes, das sich nirgendwohin bewegt, das sich einfach nur ständig wiederholt, aber sich nie zu einer Geschichte mit einem Anfang und einem Ende entwickelt. Wenn man nicht von einer Erzählung abgelenkt wird, konzentriert man sich auf das Medium selbst. Es geht darum, dass der Betrachter nicht völlig von der Illusion vereinnahmt und zu einem passiven Zuschauer wird, wie dies der Fall ist, wenn man sich im Fernsehen die Nachrichten oder eine Spieleshow ansieht. Ich fordere den Betrachter auf, sich das Videobild mit derselben kontemplativen Aufmerksamkeit anzusehen, die normalerweise der Malerei vorbehalten ist. Wenn man ein Gemälde betrachtet, dann erwartet man, dass es sich nicht bewegt; man erwartet, dass die Zeit stillsteht. Natürlich ist auch das eine Illusion. Die Zeit steht nie still. Ein Videoloop enthält das Potential, genau soviel Bewegung zu erzeugen, um die Illusion der eingefrorenen Zeit in Frage zu stellen. In praktischer Hinsicht empfinde ich den Loop als eine effektive Methode zu zeigen, wieviel Arbeit in die Herstellung des Bildes geflossen ist. Würde ich mich auf ein einzelnes Standbild aus dem Video beschränken, wäre es sehr schwierig, den Bearbeitungsaufwand zu veranschaulichen. Doch wenn man das Bild als Loop wahrnimmt, tritt der Bearbeitungsprozess wesentlich deutlicher zutage.

TR: *Caryatid* ist ein merkwürdiger Loop, weil er das Bild auf das Wesentliche reduziert. Man sieht lediglich, worum sie gekämpft haben. Du isolierst den Cup und lässt ihn schweben.

PP: Ein kleines glänzendes Etwas.

Du hast darauf hingewiesen, dass deine Arbeitsweise von deinen Lehrern beeinflusst wurde. Neben Bernd und Hilla Becher hast du Eugène Atget, August Sander und Karl Blossfeldt erwähnt. Worin

sions of the screen. That is quite a paradox, I think. Maybe the loop works similar to the shutter time in a camera. You could say that even photography is not frozen but represents the time span of the open shutter. The same time is spent in the loops, even though it is a longer time. It becomes more or less a still image.

PP: I'm not interested in using video in a narrative manner, the way video is used to make a melodrama or a documentary. I like the idea of a moving image that goes nowhere, that just repeats itself over and over again, never developing into a story line with a beginning and end. Without the distraction of a narrative, the experience stays focused on the medium itself. It's about preventing the viewer from being sucked into the illusion, becoming a passive spectator in the way people watch the news or a game show on TV. I'm asking the viewer to regard the video image with the kind of contemplative attention normally reserved for painting. When you look at a painting you expect stillness; you expect time to stop. Of course this is an illusion as well. Time never stops. With a video loop there is the potential to introduce just enough movement to create a disturbance in the illusion of frozen time. To put it in practical terms, I find the loop an effective way to foreground the labor that's gone into making the image. If I were to take a single still frame out of a video it would be very difficult to see the editing work that was done. But when you see the image looping the trace of the editing process becomes much more apparent.

TR: *Caryatid* is a strange loop because it reduces the image to the essential thing. You can only see what they have been fighting for. You isolate the cup and let it flow.

PP: A little bit of shiny something.

You've mentioned that your way of working has been influenced by your teachers. Along with Bernd and Hilla Becher, you've referenced Eugène Atget, August Sander, and Karl Blossfeldt. What do you see as the underlying commonality in these particular influences – teachers or not – on your work?

TR: What impressed me in the work of Sander, Blossfeldt, Atget and also the Bechers, is how they used the medium. They used the medium perfectly. Blossfeldt for example was not a photographer but an architecture instructor. He was teaching in Berlin and he wanted to explain to his students the differences between architectural styles. He used photography in a very straight way; he wanted to show the different archetypes of a variety of plants. And so he developed this beautiful series about them. Or let's take Hitchcock. He was a great filmmaker and in some ways an artist, not only because he made great films, but also because he used the medium in a very precise way. I think art is not reduced to the medium of painting, even though the painters still think they are the better artists.

PP: Do you mean that painters believe their medium is purer in some way?

besteht für dich die Gemeinsamkeit zwischen diesen Lehrern, die ja jeweils einen ganz spezifischen Einfluss auf dein Werk ausgeübt haben?

TR: Am Werk Sanders, Blossfeldts, Atgets und auch an dem der Bechers hat mich beeindruckt, wie sie mit dem Medium umgehen, nämlich auf perfekte Weise. Blossfeldt etwa war gar kein Fotograf, sondern unterrichtete Architektur. Er lehrte in Berlin und wollte seinen Studenten die Unterschiede zwischen verschiedenen Stilen erklären. Er setzte die Fotografie auf ganz unmittelbare Weise ein, weil er die verschiedenen Archetypen einer Reihe von Pflanzen veranschaulichen wollte. Und deshalb entwickelte er diese schöne Pflanzenserie. Oder nehmen wir Hitchcock. Er war ein großer Filmemacher und in mancher Hinsicht ein Künstler, nicht nur, weil er großartige Filme gemacht hat, sondern auch, weil er auf eine äußerst präzise Weise mit dem Medium umging. Ich denke, Kunst lässt sich nicht auf das Medium Malerei beschränken, auch wenn die Maler nach wie vor meinen, dass sie die besseren Künstler seien.

PP: Meinst du, dass die Maler glauben, ihr Medium sei irgendwie reiner?

TR: Die Malerei war das erste Medium, in dem Kunst produziert wurde, und es ist immer hart, wenn man feststellen muss, dass etwas Neues interessanter geworden ist. Aber trotzdem hängt es davon ab, wie man mit dem Medium umgeht, das man benutzt. Einer der Punkte, den mir die Bechers beibrachten, war, das Medium immer im Bild selbst zu reflektieren. Man sollte sich des Mediums immer bewusst sein, während man es benutzt. Ich denke, auch du gehst mit dem Medium auf eine sehr angemessene Weise um.

PP: Ich bemühe mich um ein aufrichtiges Verhältnis zu dem Material, das ich benutze. Das ist eine andere Möglichkeit, über den angemessenen Umgang mit dem Medium nachzudenken. Es geht darum, die Art, wie etwas funktioniert, realistisch einzuschätzen. Darum, die Sache nicht zu sehr zu forcieren, sondern sich ernsthaft zu überlegen, womit man es zu tun hat. Denkt man erst einmal darüber nach, kann das Medium Video äußerst suggestiv sein. Video ist tief in unseren Alltag eingebettet. Es reicht bis an den Kern unserer Existenz.

TR: Das Gute an der Kunstakademie in Düsseldorf war, dass ich dort mit Künstlern studierte, die andere Techniken benutzten. Meine Freunde studierten bei Bildhauern und Malern, und so lernten wir das Wesentliche der verschiedenen Medien kennen. Wir lernten, dass man eine bestimmte Idee in einer Skulptur zum Ausdruck bringen sollte, eine andere in einem Gemälde usw. Obwohl die *Substrate* sehr malerisch aussehen, sind sie keine Gemälde, sondern Computergrafiken.

PP: Die *Substrate*-Fotografien lösen bei mir etwas aus, was die meisten Computergrafiken nicht tun: Sie beschwören den Kon-

TR: It was the first medium to produce art, and it is always hard if you have to realize that something new has become more interesting. But it still depends on how you treat the medium you are using. One thing the Bechers taught me was to always reflect the medium in the image itself. You should always be aware of the medium while using it. I think that you are treating the medium also in a very proper way.

PP: I strive for an honest relationship with the material I'm using. That's another way to think about the proper treatment of the medium. It's being realistic about how things work. Not trying too hard but really considering seriously what's there. The medium of video can be very suggestive if you consider it. Video is deeply imbedded in our everyday lives. It goes to the core of our condition.

TR: The good thing at the Kunstakademie in Düsseldorf was that I was studying with artists from other disciplines. My friends were studying with sculptors and painters and so we learned the essence of the different media. We learned that this idea should be implemented by a sculpture, that one by a painting etc. Even though the *Substrates* look very much painterly, they are not paintings. They are computer graphics.

PP: One thing that the *Substrates* photographs do for me that most computer graphics don't do is activate the context of art history, the history of representation. They're beautiful images, and when I look at them I see them going back into themselves in layers. They're very slick, flat surfaces but they imply great depth. That's how I read them. What unfolds is a suggestion of the layering process it took to make them, but also how this surface relates to a whole lineage of the treatment of the picture plane. When I look at them I think of them in relation to the Internet, and I also think of them in relation to the history of painting.

TR: I thought they were mainly about taking pills. (laughter)

PP: Does this come literally into the process of experimentation for you? I think a lot of visual experiences today as being like drugs; the sheer intensity of visual stimulation possible today verges on altered states of consciousness.

TR: Did you have experiences in that way, experiences in a shift of perception or consciousness?

PP: There is an influential early experience I had when I was about ten years old, about a year after my family moved to the Philippines. Up until then we were living in Hawaii, which is tropical, but also very much an average American suburb: military bases, shopping malls, and so on. So moving to the Philippines, and specifically to an American Protestant university campus in a provincial town, was kind of a cultural shock. One day I went to sleep in a normal way. Some time in the night I woke up and felt that I was awake, but everything in my bedroom looked different. In

text der Kunstgeschichte und der Geschichte der Darstellung herauf. Es sind schöne Bilder, und wenn ich sie betrachte, sehe ich die verschiedenen Schichten, auf denen sie basieren. Es sind völlig glatte, plane Oberflächen, doch zugleich deutet sich darin eine große Tiefe an. So nehme ich sie wahr. Sie suggerieren sowohl den schichtenweisen Entstehungsprozess als auch die Tatsache, dass sich diese Oberfläche auf eine lange Tradition des Umgangs mit der Bildebene bezieht. Wenn ich sie betrachte, dann kommt mir das Internet in den Sinn, aber auch die Geschichte der Malerei.

TR: Ich dachte, es ginge bei ihnen vor allem darum, sich Pillen einzuschmeißen. (Lachen)

PP: Spielt das bei dir im Prozess des Experimentierens tatsächlich eine Rolle? Ich denke, dass viele visuelle Experimente heute wie Drogen sind. Allein die Intensität dessen, was heute an visueller Stimulation möglich ist, grenzt an veränderte Bewusstseinszustände.

TR: Hast du diesbezügliche Erfahrungen gemacht, Erfahrungen, die etwas mit einer Veränderung der Wahrnehmung oder des Bewusstseins zu tun hatten?

PP: Mit zehn hatte ich ein Erlebnis, das mich sehr beeinflusst hat. Das war etwa ein Jahr, nachdem meine Familie auf die Philippinen gezogen war. Bis dahin hatten wir in Hawai gelebt, das zwar tropisch ist, aber andererseits mehr oder weniger so wie eine durchschnittliche amerikanische Vorstadt mit Militärstützpunkten, Einkaufsarkaden usw. Der Umzug auf die Philippinen und vor allem auf den Campus einer amerikanischen protestantischen Universität in einer Provinzstadt war also eine Art Kulturschock. Eines Abends war ich ganz normal schlafen gegangen. Doch irgendwann in der Nacht, wachte ich auf und merkte, dass ich wach war. Doch in meinem Schlafzimmer sah alles ganz anders aus. Außerdem spürte ich meinen Körper nicht mehr und mein Raumgefühl hatte sich verändert. Ich hatte den Eindruck, ich sei ganz klein, das Zimmer hingegen ganz groß geworden. Ich hatte völlig die Orientierung verloren. Ich muss halb wach gewesen sein oder halb geschlafen oder geschlafwandelt haben oder irgendetwas in dieser Art. Doch damals konnte ich diese Erfahrung nicht einordnen und hatte große Angst. Da ich in die Sonntagsschule ging, war das Naheliegendste, was mir einfiel, dass ich besessen sei und sich der Teufel in meinem Zimmer befand und irgendwie in meinen Körper eingedrungen sein musste. Es kam mir vor, als sei die Grenze zwischen der Außenwelt und dem Inneren meines Körpers überschritten worden. Doch mein Grundgefühl war, dass ich besessen sei. Ich sprang aus dem Bett, verließ das Haus barfuß durch die Eingangstür und lief dem Horizont entgegen. Instinktiv lief ich in Richtung des Sonnenaufgangs und blieb erst stehen, als sich der Himmel aufzuhellen begann. Ich hatte panische Angst und versuchte instinktiv, mit Hilfe meines Sehvermögens wieder etwas

fact, I could not feel my body and my sense of space had changed. I felt like I had become very small and the space had become very big. I was completely disoriented. I must have been half-awake or half-asleep or sleepwalking or something. But at that time I had no context for this experience and it was very frightening. Because I went to Sunday school the closest thing that I could think of was that this was possession and that somehow the devil was in my room and had entered my body. I thought somehow that the boundary between the outside world and the inside of my body had been transgressed. I was possessed, basically. I jumped out of bed, walked out the front door barefoot, and just started walking away from the house and toward the horizon. I instinctively started walking in the direction of the sunrise and I did not stop walking until the sky started to become bright. It was a moment of terror and I was instinctively trying to return to some kind of stability through vision. I was looking for light so that I could make sense of what was happening to me. Actually when the sky became bright I came down from this experience. I was too freaked out to tell anybody that this happened but every night after that I had a kind of flashback. For a long time I couldn't sleep. It was really crazy because I could not tell anybody about it. So I lived with this terror for a long time. Gradually I learned to sleep in the dark again. Later, in my first year of college, I had an experience with mushrooms, which brought me very close to the experience again. As an adult, I started to think more seriously about what it means to be an artist and what is the essential point of what I am doing through art making. It is not just making pictures but it is something else. The essential project I am engaged with is to figure out if there is some way to use a tool like video or photography, which have their own rules, to develop some kind of a language to communicate this experience I had as a child, which was essentially my first experience of a kind of perceptual discovery –

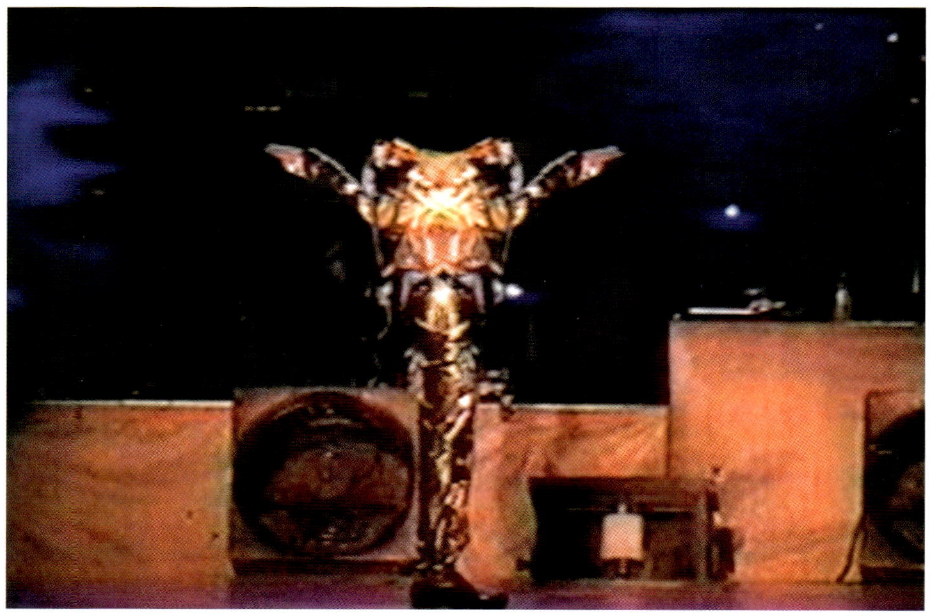

Paul Pfeiffer
Live Evil (Copenhagen), 2002
Digitaler Videoloop/digital video loop
Dimensionen variabel/
dimensions variable

Stabilität herzustellen. Ich suchte das Licht, um herauszufinden, was mit mir geschehen war. Tatsächlich endete dieses Erlebnis, als es hell wurde. Ich war viel zu verstört, als dass ich irgendjemandem davon erzählt hätte, doch anschließend hatte ich jede Nacht eine Art Flashback. Lange Zeit konnte ich überhaupt nicht schlafen. Es war wirklich verrückt, weil ich es niemandem erzählen konnte. Daher lebte ich lange Zeit mit dieser Panik. Allmählich lernte ich, wieder im Dunkeln zu schlafen. Später, während meines ersten Jahrs im College, hatte ich ein Erlebnis mit Pilzen, das dieser Erfahrung noch einmal sehr nahe kam. Als Erwachsener begann ich dann, ernsthafter darüber nachzudenken, was es heißt, ein Künstler zu sein und was eigentlich das Wesentliche ist, worum es mir geht, wenn ich Kunst mache. Es geht nicht primär um das Bildermachen, sondern um etwas anderes. Das wesentliche Projekt, mit dem ich mich befasse, ist herauszufinden, ob es eine Möglichkeit gibt, ein Instrument wie Video oder Fotografie, die ihre eigenen Regeln haben, zu benutzen, um eine Art Sprache zu entwickeln, mit der sich diese Erfahrung, die ich als Kind hatte, mitzuteilen. Für mich war dies im Wesentlichen meine erste Erfahrung mit einer Art perzeptorischer Entdeckung, nämlich der, dass die Dinge nicht das sind, was man sieht, und dass Dinge, die man für selbstverständlich hält, wie das eigene Schlafzimmer, nicht so stabil sind wie man meint. Es geht wirklich um den Versuch, die Regel zu verletzen und diese Panik wiederherzustellen, weil sich eine vertraute Wahrnehmung plötzlich verändert; es geht um diese Wiedereinführung der vierten Dimension.

Mich interessiert das, was du gerade über die Bechers gesagt hast, und diese Idee, dass man die Medien richtig oder präzise benutzen muss; aber auch, dass sie euch beigebracht haben, dass das allein nicht genügt. Bei meiner eigenen Ausbildung lag der Schwerpunkt auf der Theorie, besonders beim Whitney Independent Study Program. Das WISP gibt es seit 1968 in New York, und es hat eine gewisse Abstammungslinie aufrechterhalten. Es verlangt von denjenigen, die dieses Programm durchlaufen, die Initiation in eine bestimmte intellektuelle künstlerische Tradition. Es gibt das Klischee, dass dieses Programm die Teilnehmer zugrunde richtet, weil es zu theorielastig ist. Diejenigen, die daran teilgenommen haben, produzieren zum Schluss Werke, die in theoretischer Hinsicht sehr präzise und korrekt sind, aber nie darüber hinausgehen und daher letztlich eigentlich ziemlich uninteressant sind. Ich empfinde mich ein bisschen als etwas Besonderes, weil ich dieses Programm abgeschlossen und dennoch nicht diesen Weg eingeschlagen habe. Ich gehe zwar analytisch vor, aber letztlich ist es wichtig, loslassen zu können. Wenn ich mir deine Arbeiten ansehe, dann habe ich häufig das Gefühl, dass ich mir ein Bild ansehe und nicht begreife, wie du darauf gekommen bist. Für mich ist das wunderbar und viel interessanter, denn der

that things are not what you see and things that you take for granted, like your bedroom, may not be as stable as you think they are. It is really about trying to break the rule to recreate this terror of a familiar perception suddenly shifting, that reintroduction of the fourth dimension.

I am interested in what you said earlier about the Bechers and this idea of using the media correctly or precisely, and that they also taught that this in itself is not enough. In my own schooling there was an emphasis on theory, specifically at the Whitney Independent Study Program. The WISP has been around since 1968 in New York and has sustained a certain lineage. It demands that people who want to turn to this program become initiated into a certain intellectual legacy among artists. The stereotype of people coming out of this program is that the intense concentration on theory really destroys them. They end up making work that is theoretically very focused and correct but it never goes beyond that, and it is actually in the end quite uninteresting. I feel somewhat unique in having graduated from this program and not having taken this route. An analytical process informs me but ultimately it is important to let it go. Looking at your work I often get this feeling that I am looking at a picture and that I do not understand how you came to it. For me this is wonderful and much more interesting, as the theoretical process is very clear. I think it comes from allowing chance and intuition to enter the creative process. I am wondering how this comes into play in your work, if it does.

TR: Chance plays a very big part in my work. The human brain is too small to plan extraordinary things. If you plan something you cannot go beyond your imagination and I think art always goes beyond the limits of the imagination. So you have to take a chance and if you are lucky you get extremely interesting images. At a very early stage, when I was still a student, I had an interesting experience with chance or intuition. As I had only a little money I tried to make my photographs with one single shot. I tried to be very precise. And it always happened that either the first or the third photograph was perfect, the second never worked. I think the reason for that was that I tried to analyse what went wrong with the first shot and I then went back to the same situation in order to do it better in comparison to the first. The second one always was completely boring. After that I threw away my analysis and tried the next shot, having in mind that I did something wrong but not letting the analysis become too important. And then the third one worked. If it did not work at all, I left it alone.

PP: I think this is a really important and subtle thing. In art making it is important to respect and value an intuition. I think you can sense when something is true and when something is not true. That ultimately comes through in what you are doing.

theoretische Prozess ist ziemlich klar. Ich denke, es hat etwas damit zu tun, dass man innerhalb des kreativen Prozesses Zufall und Intuition zulässt. Ich frage mich, welche Rolle diese Faktoren in deinem Werk spielen, wenn sie eine spielen.

TR: Der Zufall spielt in meinem Werk eine sehr große Rolle. Das menschliche Gehirn ist zu klein, um außerordentliche Dinge zu planen. Wenn man etwas plant, kann man nicht über seine Einbildungskraft hinausgehen, und ich denke, Kunst geht immer über die Grenzen der Einbildungskraft hinaus. Man muss sich also auf ein Risiko einlassen, und wenn man Glück hat, führt das zu äußerst interessanten Bildern. Zu einem sehr frühen Zeitpunkt, als ich noch Student war, machte ich eine interessante Erfahrung mit Zufall oder Intuition. Da ich sehr wenig Geld hatte, versuchte ich meine Fotografien mittels einer einzigen Aufnahme zu machen. Ich versuchte, sehr genau zu sein. Und es war immer so, dass entweder die erste oder die dritte Aufnahme perfekt war, aber nie die zweite. Ich denke das lag daran, dass ich versuchte festzustellen, was bei der ersten Aufnahme schief gegangen war und dann noch einmal auf dieselbe Situation zurückkam, um sie im Vergleich zur ersten besser zu machen. Die zweite war immer total langweilig. Danach verzichtete ich auf die Analyse und machte die nächste Aufnahme, wobei ich immer daran dachte, dass ich etwas falsch gemacht hatte, aber zugleich darauf achtete, dass die Analyse nicht die Oberhand gewann. Und die dritte Aufnahme funktionierte dann. Wenn gar nichts ging, ließ ich es bleiben.

PP: Ich glaube, das ist wirklich eine wichtige und subtile Sache. Bei der Kunstproduktion ist es wichtig, die Intuition zu achten und zu schätzen. Ich denke, man spürt, wann etwas stimmt und wann nicht. Letztlich zeigt sich das in dem, was man macht.

Meinst du, dass sich zwischen dem Zeitpunkt, als du deine ersten reifen Fotografien gemacht hast und heute das Medium Fotografie oder der Kontext für die Verwendung der Fotografie als Werkzeug verändert hat?

TR: Ja. Das ist einer der Gründe, warum ich meinen Studenten nicht sage, was sie tun sollen oder welche Technik sie benutzen sollen. Sie sind völlig anders aufgewachsen als meine Generation, und sie benutzen ein völlig anderes Vokabular als ich. Ich möchte nicht sagen »Das ist falsch« oder »Du musst das so oder so machen.« Sie müssen das selbst entwickeln. Dein Werk wäre vor zwanzig Jahren noch nicht möglich gewesen, weder in technischer Hinsicht noch im Hinblick darauf, wie man dieses Werk auffasst. Ich glaube wirklich, dass jede Generation ihren eigenen Ausdruck hat.

PP: Meinst du, dass das teilweise damit zusammenhängt, dass immer mehr Instrumente für die Bildproduktion zur Verfügung stehen?

Do you think the medium of photography, or the context for the usage of photography as a tool has shifted from when you were making your first mature photographs to today?

TR: Yes. This is one reason why I wont tell my students what to do or what technique they should use. They have grown up completely different to my generation and they have a completely different vocabulary than I have for my work. I do not want to say »You are wrong,« or »You have to do it this or that way.« They have to develop it by themselves. Your work would not have been possible twenty years ago, in terms of technique and also in terms of what to think about the work. I really believe that every generation has its own expression.

PP: Do you think it has partially to do with the increased availability or access to tools for image making?

TR: Definitely. My generation grew up with TV, magazines and a lot of photographic images. A hundred years ago there was probably a painting on the wall or an etching or some other kind of reproduction. For my generation or maybe also for the generation before me it was quite natural to pick up the camera and try to explain our life, our world. Video was fascinating for me but technically very tricky. The next generation, and I guess one could include you, had access to simpler techniques, and so they could start to work in a more playful way with it.

PP: I put less emphasis on technique per se. Maybe I am closer to your generation in my thinking about this. It is important to be honest about the nature of the material, especially when you are dealing with a production system that has a lot to do with fashion and advertising. To me the issue of the artist's hand is less important than the idea that there are these amazing tools out there that are almost exclusively being used by the mass marketing industries. The aims of the artist are almost the antithesis of advertising. It is a little bit frustrating to me when I talk about my work; people want to know what software I use. They gravitate immediately to the technical details. In fact, I realize I have been attempting to keep my editing process very simple. I use basic desktop software and the alterations I make to the original image are labor-intensive but visually minimal, like painting out the boxers in the ring, or centering an element in the frame that was originally in the margins of the shot. Keeping it basic allows the viewer to focus on the manipulation that's taken place. The manipulation becomes something like the subject of the work.

TR: If you erase for example Muhammad Ali, do you do it by yourself or do you have somebody who does that?

PP: I did the first *Long Count* video with the help of a friend of mine, who is actually my oldest friend from art school. There were at least three other people in the studio helping out, but it was really Aaron and myself who were the most

TR: Ganz bestimmt. Meine Generation wuchs mit dem Fernseher, mit Zeitschriften und vielen Fotografien auf. Vor hundert Jahren hing stattdessen wahrscheinlich ein Gemälde an der Wand oder eine Radierung oder irgendeine andere Reproduktion. Für meine Generation oder vielleicht auch für die Generation vor mir war es ganz natürlich, sich die Kamera zu schnappen und zu versuchen, unser Leben, unsere Welt zu erklären. Video war faszinierend für mich, doch in technischer Hinsicht sehr kompliziert. Die nächste Generation, und ich meine, man kann dich dazuzählen, hatte Zugang zu einfacheren Techniken, so dass sie anfangen konnte, auf spielerischere Weise damit zu arbeiten.

PP: Ich habe weniger Gewicht auf die Technik an sich gelegt. Vielleicht stehe ich hinsichtlich meines Denkens in diesem Punkt deiner Generation näher. Es ist wichtig, der Natur des Materials gegenüber aufrichtig zu sein, vor allem wenn man es mit einem Produktionssystem zu tun hat, das viel mit Mode und Werbung zu tun hat. Für mich ist die Frage der Handschrift des Künstlers weniger wichtig als die Idee, dass es da all diese verblüffenden Werkzeuge gibt, die fast ausschließlich von den Marketing-Großindustrien benutzt werden. Die Ziele des Künstlers sind der Werbung nahezu diametral entgegengesetzt. Es ist ein bisschen frustrierend für mich, dass die Leute, wenn ich über meine Werke spreche, wissen wollen, welche Software ich benutze. Die kommen immer sofort auf die technischen Details zu sprechen. Tatsächlich stelle ich fest, dass ich versucht habe, den Bearbeitungsprozess so einfach wie möglich zu gestalten. Ich benutze einfache Desktop-Software und die Änderungen, die ich an dem ursprünglichen Bild vornehme sind zwar sehr arbeitsintensiv, aber in visueller Hinsicht minimal; etwa wenn ich die Boxer im Ring übermale oder ein Bildelement in den Mittelpunkt rücke, das sich ursprünglich am Rand des Bildes befand. Indem man sich auf das Grundlegende beschränkt, ermöglicht man es dem Betrachter, sich auf die Manipulation zu konzentrieren, die stattgefunden hat. Die Manipulation wird gewissermaßen zum Sujet des Werks.

TR: Wenn du zum Beispiel Muhammad Ali aus dem Bild entfernst, machst du das dann selbst, oder hast du jemanden, der das für dich erledigt?

PP: Das erste *Long Count*-Video habe ich mit Hilfe eines Freundes gemacht, der übrigens mein ältester Freund von der Kunsthochschule ist. Mindestens drei andere Leute im Studio haben uns ebenfalls geholfen, aber Aaron und ich waren diejenigen, die am stärksten daran interessiert waren, die Sache zu einem Abschluss zu bringen. Wir haben ungefähr vier Monate benötigt und dabei mindestens acht Stunden am Tag gearbeitet; wir hatten also eine Vierzig-Stunden-Woche. Bei diesem Verfahren wird nämlich Bild für Bild bearbeitet. Nach dieser Erfahrung war mein erster Gedanke, dass ich

focused about completing this. It took us about four months working at least eight hours a day, like a forty hour week. Because the nature of it is that it is frame-by-frame editing. After this experience my immediate thought was that I have to find some special effects company that can do this for us. I took my sample around to several big post-production houses in New York and London. They came back to me and said, »There is no other software to do this other than the one you are using and to be honest, if you give it to us, we will do the same thing you are doing but we will charge you ten times as much.« So I was stuck. I have been working like this since then. I think the only route to go is to develop the infrastructure necessary for this project by myself, not that it has to be done by myself. I am building up a team of people who I know and trust and who can work with me in this way. Recently I brought a professional special effects postproduction editor into my studio. He does commercials and has done work on movies like the more recent *Alien* movies. I brought him in because I wanted to get his advice about some pieces I am working on now. I showed him several different videos and asked him what he thought. I was treating him like a consultant and he had some very interesting timesaving ideas for each one of the projects. That made me realize it could be very fruitful to work with somebody like this. By extension it means the possibility to me of accessing what is essentially the advertising industry's system of production and having a dialogue with this existing work force to do something which is in some ways very simple compared to what they usually do but also very different. What I am looking for are tools that are basic compared to what an advertiser is looking for. But I am also looking for this relationship where the people that I work with understand the nature of what we are doing and how it departs from the standard usage of the system.

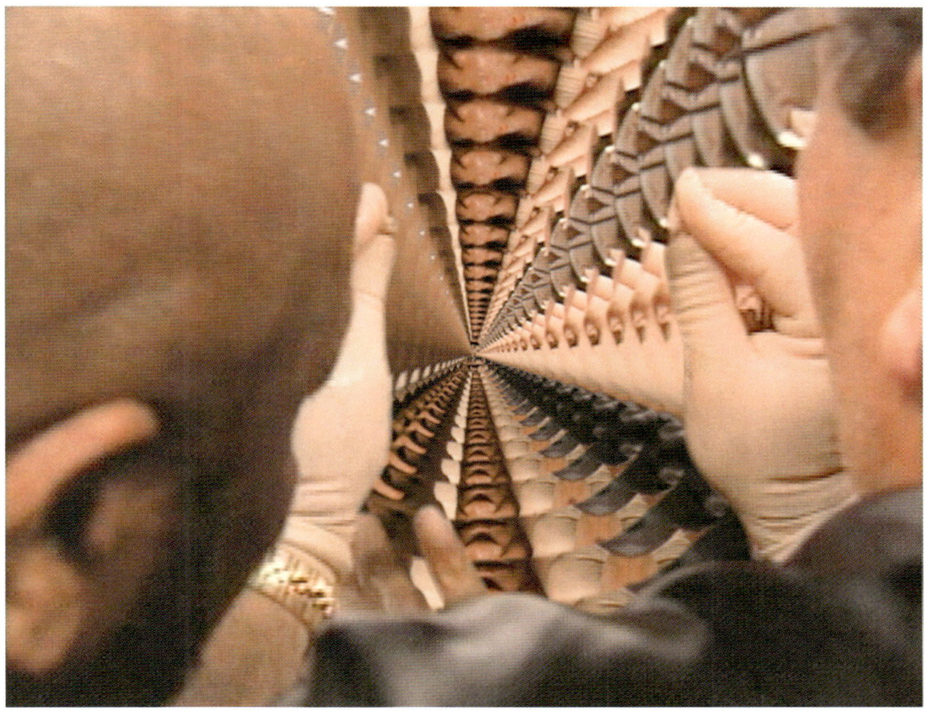

Paul Pfeiffer
Corner Piece, 2002
Digitaler Videoloop mit Ton /
Digital video loop with sound
Dimensionen variabel /
Dimensions variable

eine Special Effects-Firma finden müsste, die das für uns erledigen kann. Ich habe meine Probe verschiedenen Post-Production-Firmen in New York und London gezeigt. Die haben sich dann wieder bei mir gemeldet und gesagt: »Es gibt keine andere Software dafür als die, die Sie benutzen, und um ehrlich zu sein, wenn Sie uns den Auftrag erteilen, dann werden wir dasselbe machen wie Sie, nur dass wir Ihnen dafür das Zehnfache in Rechnung stellen.« Ich steckte also fest. Seither habe ich immer so gearbeitet. Ich denke, meine einzige Möglichkeit ist, die Infrastruktur für dieses Projekt selbst zu entwickeln, auch wenn ich sie vielleicht nicht selbst herstellen muss. Ich baue mir ein Team von Leuten auf, die ich kenne und denen ich vertrauen kann und die auf diese Weise mit mir zusammenarbeiten können. Vor Kurzem habe ich mir einen professionellen Post-Production-Editor für Special Effects ins Studio geholt. Er macht Werbespots und hat an Projekten wie den letzten *Alien*-Filmen mitgearbeitet. Ich habe ihn kommen lassen, weil ich seinen Ratschlag zu einigen Werken haben wollte, an denen ich gerade arbeite. Ich zeigte ihm verschiedene Videos und fragte ihn nach seiner Meinung. Ich habe ihn wie einen Berater behandelt und er hatte zu jedem der Projekte einige sehr interessante Ideen, mit denen sich Zeit sparen ließ. Da wurde mir klar, dass es sehr ergiebig sein könnte, mit so jemandem zusammenzuarbeiten. Darüber hinaus böte es mir Gelegenheit, Zugang zu einem Produktionssystem zu finden, das im Wesentlichen das der Werbeindustrie ist, und in einen Dialog mit dieser bereits existierenden Größe zu treten. So könnte man etwas machen, das in mancher Hinsicht sehr einfach ist im Vergleich zu dem, was dort normalerweise gemacht wird, aber zugleich auch ganz anders. Ich suche nach Instrumenten, die im Vergleich zu dem, wonach ein Werber sucht, ziemlich einfach sind. Aber ich suche auch nach einer Beziehung, bei der die Leute, für die ich arbeite, den Charakter dessen verstehen, was wir machen, und begreifen, inwieweit es von der üblichen Verwendungsweise des Systems abweicht.

TR: Wie denkst du über Autorschaft? Es gibt bei dir mehrere unterschiedliche Werke wie *Orpheus Descending* oder *Morning after the Deluge*, die du wahrscheinlich selbst aufgenommen hast. Andere wie das *Long Count*-Video oder die Szene, in der Tom Cruise auf dem Sofa liegt, konntest du nicht selber drehen. Welche Beziehung besteht zwischen fremdem Material und Material, das du selber aufgenommen hast?

PP: Für mich macht das keinen Unterschied. Ob man in der Post-Produktion Archivmaterial bearbeitet oder Originalaufnahmen macht, das Problem ist immer dasselbe, das heißt, das Material ist immer schon mit Bedeutung befrachtet, bevor man versucht, es einzusetzen. Jedes neue Bild ist durch die gesamte Geschichte der Bilder bedingt, die ihm vorausgehen. Jedes Videobild ist durch die Geschich-

TR: What about your ideas of authorship? You have several different works, like *Orpheus Descending* or *Morning after the Deluge*, which you probably have shot yourself. Others like the *Long Count* or the scene where Tom Cruise is on the sofa you could not shoot yourself. What is the relation between appropriated material and material you have shot by yourself? Is there a difference?

PP: To me there is no difference. Whether you are doing postproduction work on archival material or shooting original footage, to me the problem is always the same: the material is already loaded with meaning before you try to use it. Every new image is conditioned by the entire history of images that comes before it. Every video image is conditioned by the history of the medium, and by its primary usage in the broadcasting industry. It's the same tools used by advertising agencies and blockbuster moviemakers. Digital imaging is the language of today's global monoculture. My thought process is closer to my background in printmaking then advertising. I got into printmaking because I was really interested in the process, the nature of this medium that is essentially mechanically reproduced. I like the idea of the author being something like a director and that the manual process starts from an analysis of what already exists. Understanding that the artist is attempting to use tools that are not really meant for that kind of work, it becomes more like an act of directing and translating and less about originality. The idea that the artist is doing everything, the idea of the whole production taking place within one human body seems to be archaic and actually uninteresting. It occurs to me that if you think of advertising as based around the celebrity or the personality of somebody who is selling a product, all the tools are used to build up the image of this recognizable person who becomes the face of the product. In actuality it has very little to do with the manufacture of the product. Making videos where I am essentially erasing a celebrity, I am leaving all the stuff that is around the celebrity in place. Maybe in a similar way I am trying to do the same thing in relation to this tradition of the artist being the author. I'm using this myth for my own purposes. Hopefully I am being smart enough to realize that it is just a myth. In the end, I hope that does not sound too cynical. It is very difficult to work in today's world without having some kind of confrontation with the system of image making for mass marketing. I am afraid that even in the art world the way people think has been highly influenced by the entertainment and advertising industries. For me it is just a matter of being smart enough to understand how it works and to understand that there is actually much more that is going on than just the use of the eye. It is a funny contradiction. Both in advertising and in the art world there is this insistence on locating one individual as the focus of attention. It is both frightening and exciting. It is important for people who are engaged in not just selling but experimenting to access this system. Advertisers are

te des Mediums bedingt und dadurch, dass es primär in der Film- und Fernsehindustrie verwendet wird. Es handelt sich um dieselben Werkzeuge, die auch von Werbeagenturen und Blockbuster produzierenden Filmemachern verwendet werden. Die digitale Bilderzeugung ist die Sprache der heutigen globalen Monokultur. Mein Denken ist eher von der Druckgrafik geprägt, von der ich herkomme, als durch die Werbung. Ich habe mich deshalb mit der Herstellung von Druckgrafiken beschäftigt, weil ich mich wirklich für den Prozess interessiert habe, für die Natur dieses Mediums, das im Wesentlichen mechanisch reproduziert wird. Mir gefiel die Vorstellung, dass der Autor so etwas wie ein Regisseur ist und dass der manuelle Prozess mit einer Analyse des Vorhandenen beginnt. Wenn man begreift, dass der Künstler versucht, Instrumente zu benutzen, die nicht wirklich für diese Art von Werken gedacht sind, geht es dabei mehr um einen Akt des Regieführens und Übersetzens und weniger um Originalität. Die Idee, dass der Künstler alles macht, die Idee, dass die gesamte Produktion innerhalb eines menschlichen Körpers stattfindet, wirkt archaisch und ist de facto uninteressant. Wenn man wie ich der Meinung ist, dass Werbung sich um die Prominenz oder die Persönlichkeit von jemandem dreht, der ein Produkt verkauft, dann sieht man, dass sämtliche Instrumente dazu benutzt werden, das Image dieser wiedererkennbaren Person aufzubauen, die dem Produkt ein Gesicht verleiht. Tatsächlich hat das sehr wenig mit der Herstellung des Produktes selbst zu tun. Bei den Videos, die im Wesentlichen darin bestehen, dass ich einen Prominenten entferne, lasse ich das ganze Drumherum da, wo es ist. Vielleicht versuche ich im Hinblick auf die Tradition, derzufolge der Künstler der Autor ist, dasselbe auf ähnliche Art zu machen. Ich nutze diesen Mythos für meine eigenen Zwecke. Hoffentlich bin ich schlau genug, um zu realisieren, dass es sich nur um einen Mythos handelt. Ich hoffe, dass das jetzt nicht zu zynisch klingt. Es ist sehr schwierig, in der Welt von heute zu arbeiten, ohne irgendwie mit der Bildproduktion für das Massenmarketing in Berührung zu kommen. Ich befürchte, dass sogar in der Welt der Kunst die Denkweise der Leute sehr stark von der Unterhaltungs- und Werbeindustrie beeinflusst wurde. Für mich geht es einfach darum, schlau genug zu sein, um zu begreifen, wie das funktioniert und dass es dabei um viel mehr geht als nur den Einsatz der Augen. Das ist ein lustiger Widerspruch. Sowohl in der Werbung als auch in der Welt der Kunst gibt es dieses Beharren darauf, dass ein Individuum im Mittelpunkt der Aufmerksamkeit steht. Das ist sowohl beängstigend als auch aufregend. Es ist wichtig, dass Leute, die sich nicht nur mit dem Verkauf beschäftigen, sondern experimentieren, Zugang zu diesem System haben. Werber interessieren sich nur für einen kleinen Prozentsatz des wirklichen Potentials dieser Instrumente, nämlich den, den man benötigt, um ein Produkt zu verkau-

only interested in using a small percentage of the real potential of the tools, basically, to sell a product. It's only with artists that the tools can be harnessed back to what I think are their real potential. I think advertising, Hollywood and industries like them will always be able to do most things better than artists. But there is one thing that they can never do that the artist can do: tailor a visual experience to a single person rather than a mass audience. I don't like the black box solution for presenting video. It is too much like a movie theater. In the black box environment everything disappears, your body disappears, the whole sense of reality disappears and all you are left with is an illusion that your eye is drawn into. Then the movie ends and you are left with nothing. The one thing that a movie could never do which an artist can potentially do with this kind of medium is to include some awareness of the medium itself and incorporate physicality in the experience, some kind of deeper awareness of what is happening when you are going through this visual mental shift.

TR: I must confess that I have never thought about that problem. I thought of photography as a very traditional medium for the arts. Even though new tools appear, I am still working on photographic images. If I can not take the photograph by myself, I have to find somewhere else, in case of the *Stars* from an astronomical observatory, in the case of the *nudes* on the porn pages in the World Wide Web, in the case of the *Newspaper Photographs* in the newspaper itself etc. I think you must have a similar experience. The things you can shoot yourself, you shoot yourself. Things you cannot shoot yourself you have to get from somewhere. Then altering things is part of the artistic practice.

PP: But if you think of the social context for the tool, this is changing. The way that I see it changing is that digital imaging tools are gaining a monopoly over people's attention and experience. I am doing my own thing, which is a much small-

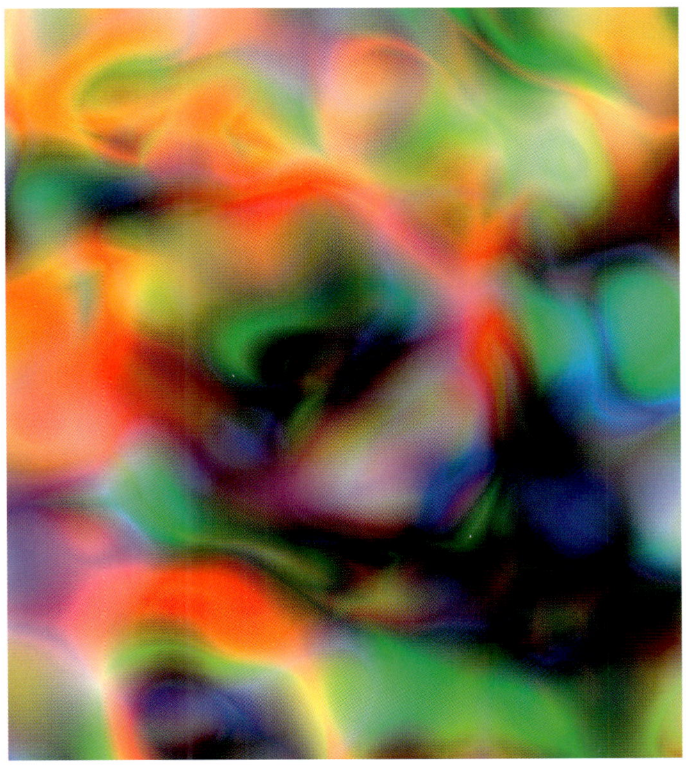

Thomas Ruff
Substrat 18 III, 2003
C-Print
186 x 204 cm

fen. Ich denke, nur durch Künstler können diese Instrumente wieder so genutzt werden, dass sie ihr volles Potential entfalten. Ich glaube, dass Hollywood und vergleichbare Industrien immer in der Lage sein werden, die meisten Dinge besser zu machen als ein Künstler. Aber es gibt eine Sache, zu der sie im Gegensatz zu einem Künstler nie imstande sein werden, nämlich eine visuelle Erfahrung auf eine einzelne Person zuzuschneiden statt auf ein Massenpublikum. Ich präsentiere Videos ungern in einer Black Box. Das ist zu sehr wie Kino. Im Kontext der Black Box verschwindet alles, nicht nur der Körper, sondern das ganze Wirklichkeitsgefühl, und das Einzige, was übrig bleibt, ist eine Illusion, in die dein Auge hineingezogen wird. Dann ist der Film zu Ende und alles ist vorbei. Das Einzige, wozu ein Film nie imstande ist, aber was ein Künstler mit dieser Art Medium tun könnte, ist das Bewusstsein für das Medium selbst miteinzubeziehen und Körperlichkeit in diese Erfahrung zu inkorporieren, eine Art tieferes Bewusstsein dafür, was passiert, wenn man diese visuelle mentale Veränderung durchläuft.

TR: Ich muss gestehen, dass ich nie über dieses Problem nachgedacht habe. Ich habe Fotografie immer als ein sehr traditionelles Medium für die Kunst empfunden. Auch wenn neue Instrumente auftauchen, arbeite ich doch mit fotografischen Bildern. Wenn ich die Aufnahme nicht selber machen kann, muss ich sie mir irgendwoanders besorgen, im Fall der *Sterne* über ein astronomisches Observatorium, im Fall der *nudes* von den Pornoseiten im Internet, im Fall der *Zeitungsfotos* aus der Zeitung selbst usw. Ich nehme an, dass du ähnliche Erfahrungen gemacht hast. Was du selbst aufnehmen kannst, nimmst du selber auf. Was du nicht selbst aufnehmen kannst, besorgst du dir woanders. Diese Bilder dann zu verändern ist Teil der künstlerischen Praxis.

PP: Aber der gesellschaftliche Kontext des Instruments verändert sich. Meines Erachtens verändert er sich dahingehend, dass die Instrumente der digitalen Bildbearbeitung ein Monopol über die Aufmerksamkeit und Erfahrung der Menschen gewinnen. Ich mache mein eigenes Ding, das im Vergleich zur Werbeindustrie ein wesentlich kleineres und idiosynkratischeres Projekt ist; es ist sehr arrogant, wenn ich mich mit der Werbeindustrie vergleiche, weil sie in einem völlig anderen Maßstab arbeitet, aber aus irgendeinem Grund tue ich es trotzdem. Ich bin mir stets im Klaren darüber, dass die Werbeindustrie das ist, wogegen ich ankämpfe. Ich bediene mich gewissermaßen der Instrumente des Gegners. Vielleicht klingt das wirklich allzu simpel und paranoid, aber mir schwebt der Mensch vor, der sich letztlich entscheidet, ob er sich etwas im Fernsehen oder in einer Galerie ansieht. Irgendwie stelle ich mir vor, dass ich gegen einen Feind ankämpfe.

er and idiosyncratic project compared to the advertising industry; it is quite arrogant to compare myself to the advertising industry because its scale is so different but for some reason I do. I am constantly aware that this is what I am fighting against. I am using the tools of the enemy in a way. Perhaps that sounds really simplistic and paranoid but I have the person in mind that is ultimately going to decide to watch something on TV or look at something in a gallery. I suppose in some way I do fight against an enemy.

TR: At first I am not working for an audience. It is my curiosity that makes me develop a series. I am not thinking then about how the work will be received by an audience. But of course I am very happy if the work is also interesting for others.

PP: Most images are produced in millions and circulated globally. So an artist's edition of three or five or twenty is ridiculously small by comparison. It is a crucial difference because again it is going back to an understanding that we are working in video or photography in relation to a much bigger distribution system. The question is how to distinguish your project or my project from the bigger project, especially if I am using images that in some way are very similar to the bigger project. I think it is simply this aspect of refusing to let the image enter into the larger circulation system. I remember I was told that it seemed like a shame to be working in this very populist medium of video and yet making this work that is going to be seen by a very small quantity of people and only in this very precise condition. Not on TV, not on a big screen, but only in a gallery and always in this same specific physical relation to the viewer. My response was that this is exactly the point. Most images in the world are produced for a mass audience and we do not need any more images of this kind. It is redundant to try to make more images to circulate in the system. So it seems like a very precious thing to still have the option in this world to make images in what is the extension of a much older context, the context of painting where you always have the essential relationship between the painting and one viewer, not a million viewers. Reproductions can still be circulated through magazines but the piece itself is always brought back to this very archaic relationship which otherwise does not exist in the world anymore. The benefits of this older system are that there are degrees of depth and nuance and subtlety of communication with a single viewer that can happen in the context of art that are impossible in the context of mass media.

TR: Zunächst arbeite ich nicht für ein Publikum. Es ist meine Neugier, die mich eine Serie entwickeln lässt. Ich denke dann nicht darüber nach, wie das Werk vom Publikum aufgenommen werden wird. Aber natürlich freue ich mich, wenn das Werk auch für andere interessant ist.

PP: Die meisten Bilder werden millionenfach produziert und zirkulieren weltweit. Im Vergleich dazu ist eine Auflage von drei oder fünf oder zwanzig Bildern für ein Kunstwerk lächerlich klein. Das ist ein wesentlicher Unterschied, weil er wieder zu der Einsicht zurückführt, dass wir mit Video oder Fotografie im Verhältnis zu einem wesentlich größeren Distributionssystem arbeiten. Die Frage ist, wie man dein Projekt oder mein Projekt von dem größeren Projekt unterscheiden kann, vor allem dann, wenn man Bilder verwendet, die in mancher Hinsicht dem größeren Projekt sehr ähneln. Ich denke, es ist einfach dieser Aspekt, dass man sich weigert, das Bild in diesen größeren Kreislauf eintreten zu lassen. Ich erinnere mich, dass man mir gesagt hat, es sei fast eine Schande, mit diesem äußerst populistischen Medium Video zu arbeiten und dennoch solche Arbeiten zu machen, die nur von einer ganz begrenzten Anzahl von Menschen und nur unter genau diesen Bedingungen betrachtet werden. Nicht im Fernsehen, nicht auf einer großen Leinwand, sondern nur in einer Galerie und immer im selben spezifischen physischen Verhältnis zum Betrachter. Meine Antwort darauf lautete, dass es mir genau darum geht. Die meisten Bilder in der Welt werden für ein Massenpublikum produziert, und wir benötigen keine weiteren Bilder dieser Art. Es ist überflüssig zu versuchen, noch mehr Bilder im System zirkulieren zu lassen. Es scheint mir daher etwas sehr Kostbares zu sein, in dieser Welt noch immer die Option zu haben, Bilder in der Erweiterung eines wesentlich älteren Kontexts zu machen, nämlich dem der Malerei, wo man immer die wesentliche Beziehung zwischen dem Gemälde und einem Betrachter und nicht Millionen Betrachtern hat. Abbildungen können nach wie vor durch Zeitschriften zirkulieren, aber das Werk selbst wird immer wieder auf diese archaische Beziehung zurückgeführt, die es sonst nirgendwo in der Welt mehr gibt. Die Vorzüge dieses älteren Systems bestehen darin, dass es verschiedene Grade von Tiefe, Nuanciertheit und Subtilität von Kommunikation mit einem einzelnen Betrachter gibt, die sich im Kontext der Kunst ereignen können, während sie im Kontext der Massenmedien unmöglich sind.

Übersetzung aus dem Englischen: Nikolaus G. Schneider

BIOGRAFIE UND AUSBILDUNG/
BIOGRAPHY AND EDUCATION

Paul Pfeiffer
Geboren 1966 in Honolulu, Hawaii
Lebt und arbeitet in New York

Born 1966 in Honolulu, Hawaii
Lives and works in New York

1987
BFA, San Francisco Art Institute

1994
MFA, Hunter College, New York

1997-98
Whitney Museum of American Art Independent Study Program

AUSZEICHNUNGEN UND STIPENDIEN /
AWARDS AND SCHOLARSHIPS

1991-92
Barbara Smith Artist Trust

1993
Travel Grant Pilot, National Endowment for the Arts and Art International

1994
Project Grant, Art Matters

1994-95
Fulbright-Hayes Fellowship to the Philippines

1999
World Trade Center Residency, Lower Manhatten Cultural Council, New York

1999-2000
Public Art Fund, New York

2000
The Bucksbaum Award, Whitney Museum of American Art
Travel Grant, Asian Cultural Council

2001-02
MIT List Visual Arts Center Residency, Cambridge

2003
ArtPace Residency, San Antonio

EINZELAUSSTELLUNGEN /
SOLO EXHIBITIONS

1993
Survival of the Innocents, Art In General, New York

1994
Santo Niño Incarnate Colonial House Inn, New York

1997
The Pure Products Go Crazy, Cendrillon, New York

1998
The Pure Products Go Crazy, The Project, New York

2000
Duke University Museum of Art, Raleigh-Durham, North Carolina (with Romuald Hazoumé)
The Project, New York
Kunst-Werke, Berlin

2001
Barbican Art Centre, London
Kunsthaus Glarus, Glarus
Sex Machine, The Project, Los Angeles
Orpheus Descending, Public Art Fund, World Trade & Financial Centers, New York (Kat./cat.)
UCLA Hammer, Los Angeles, California
Whitney Museum of American Art, New York

2003
MIT, List Visual Art Centre, Cambridge, MA; Museum of Contemporary Art, Chicago; The Contemporary Museum, Honolulu, Hawaii (Kat./cat.)
Gio Marconi, Milan, Italy

2004
K 21 Kunstsammlung Nordrhein-Westfalen, Düsseldorf (Kat./cat.)

GRUPPENAUSSTELLUNGEN (AUSWAHL) /
SELECTED GROUP EXHIBITIONS

1991
Dismantling Invisibility: Asian Americans Respond to the AIDS Crisis, Art In General, New York

1992
Altars, Divinations and Icons, Painted Bride Art Center, Philadelphia; Guadalupe Cultural Center, San Antonio, (Kat./cat.)
(en)Gendered Visions: Race, Gender and Sexuality in Asian American Art
Injustice, Guadalupe Cultural Center, San Antonio, (Kat./cat.)
Made in America: Remembering Vincent Chin, Art In General, New York

1993
The Curio Shop, Artists Space, New York (Kat./cat.)
Kayumanggi Presence, Academy of Art, Honolulu

1994
Extreme Unction, Market Gallery, London (Kat./cat.)
Reframing a Heritage, University Of Hawaii, Manoa, Hawaii
Stonewalls, 494 Gallery, New York
Picturing Asia America: Communities, Cultures, Difference, Houston Center for Photography, Houston

1995
In a Different Light, UC Berkeley Museum, Berkeley (Kat./cat.)
Pervert, UC Irvine Art Gallery, Irvine (Kat./cat.)
14 Artist: Sugod sa Katapusan, End House Art Center, Dumaguete City, Philippines

1996
Memories of Overdevelopment: Philippine Diaspora in Contemporary Art, UC Irvine Art Gallery, Irvine; Plug-In Gallery, Winnipeg, Canada (1997) (Kat./cat.)
Neighbors, Boom Gallery, Honolulu

1997
Travel Size, City College, New York
Fermented, Parsons School of Design, New York

1998
warming, The Project, New York
At Home and Abroad: 21 Contemporary Filipino Artists, Asian Art Museum, San Francisco (Kat./cat.)

1999
Tete de Turkois, The Project, New York
Surface Tension, Art in General, New York
A Place Called Lovely, Greene Naftali, New York
Hocus Focus: New Video, Rare Gallery, New York

2000
The Whitney Biennial, The Whitney Museum of American Art, New York (Kat./cat.)
Greater New York, P.S.1 Contemporary Art Center, New York, (Kat./cat.)
Hypermental, Kunsthaus, Zürich; Hamburger Kunsthalle (2001) (Kat./cat.)
City Visions, media city_seoul 2000, Seoul, Korea
Extraordinary Realities, Columbus Museum of Art, Columbus, Ohio
Scanner, Oliver Art Center, California College of Art & Culture, Oakland, CA

2001
Plateau der Menschheit, 49. Biennale von Venedig, Venedig (Kat./cat.)
Bitstreams, Whitney Museum of American Art, New York
Gio Marconi, Mailand
Maze Gallery, Turin
Sala Uno, Rom
Casino 2001, SMAK, Gent (Kat./cat.)
Zero Gravity, Rom (Kat./cat.)
The Americans, Barbican Arts Centre, London (Kat./cat.)
Subject Plural, Museum of Contemporary Art, Houston (Kat./cat.)
Refresh, Cantor Centre for the Visual Arts
Monitor: Volume One, Gagosian Gallery, New York
Silliman University, Philippines
Passion, Ascan Crone, Hamburg
Race in Digital Space, MIT List Visual Art Center, Cambridge
Loop, Kunsthalle der Hypokultursiftung, München; P.S.1, New York (Kat./cat.)
Metropolis 2002, Istanbul
MIT List Visual Arts Center, Cambridge
False Start, Center for Curatorial Studies, Bard College, Annandale-on-Hudson, NY
American Art From the Goetz Collection, Galerie Rudolfinum, Prag (Kat./cat.)

2002
Out of Place: Contemporary Art and the Architectural Uncanny, Museum of Contemporary Art, Chicago (Kat./cat.)
Pictures, Greene Naftali, New York
Model World, The Aldrich Contemporary Art Museum, Ridgefield (Kat./cat.)
The Beach, Winsor on Vero Beach, Florida (Kat./cat.)
Tempo, Museum of Modern Art, New York (Kat./cat.)
Busan Biennale, Busan, Korea
Startkapital, Eröffnungspräsentation/inaugural exhibition K21 Kunstsammlung Nordrhein-Westfalen, Düsseldorf (Kat./cat.)
Special Effects (2002 Media Art), Daejeon Municipal Museum of Art, Korea
One Hand Clapping, Smackmelon, Brooklyn
NYC Sex, Museum of Sex, New York
Miami Currents: Linking Collection & Community, Miami Art Museum, Miami
Interplay, The Moore Building, Miami

2003
Cairo Biennial 2003, The Palace of Fine Art, Kairo (Kat./cat.)
Postproduction from Collage to Sampling, Dundee Contemporary Arts, Dundee
100 Artists See God, Independent Curators International, New York (touring USA)
Black Belt, The Studio Museum in Harlem, New York
Fast Forward – Media Art, Sammlung Goetz, ZKM Zentrum für Kunst und Medientechnologie, Karlsruhe (Kat./cat.)
Nuit Blanche Museum of Contemporary Art of the City of Paris, Paris
A Simple Plan, James Cohan Gallery, New York
Uneasy Space, SITE Santa Fe, Santa Fe
The Squared Circle: Boxing in Contemporary Art, Walker Art Center, Minneapolis
The Moderns, Castello di Rivoli, Turin
Graz 2003 (As Heavy as the Heavens), Graz
Losing It, Fenton Gallery, Cork
Social Strategies: Redefining Social Realism, University of California, Los Angeles
American Dream, Ronald Feldman Gallery, New York

2004
Eclipse Towards the edge of the visible, White Cube, London
Phantasmagoria, Butler Museum of American Arts Beecher Center of Art and Technology, Youngstown
Size Matters, Independent Curators International, New York
Die zehn Gebote, Hygiene Museum, Dresden (Kat./cat.)
Faces in the Crowd: The Modern Figure and Avant-Grande Realism, Whitechapel Art Gallery, London
Contested Fields: Identity in Sports and Spectacle, Des Moines Art Center, Des Moines
Modern Means: Continuity and Change in Art, 1880 to the Present, Mori Art Museum, Tokyo

Bibliography of Asian American Artists. Unveröffentlichte Studie in den Archiven des Asian American Studies Center, Queens Collage, New York / Unpublished research paper in the archives of the Asian American Studies Center, Queens College, New York, 1992

»Out In the 90s«, *Godzilla: The Magazine of the Asian American Artists Network*, Vol. 2, no. 1, Summer 1992

»Our Lady of Perpetual Health«, *Lavender Godzilla: Voices of Gay Asian & Pacific Islander Men*, San Francisco, CA, Fall 1992

»Is There An Asian American Aesthetic?«, *Artspiral*, Asian American Arts Center, New York, Fall 1992

Artist portfolio. *MUAE II: Collapsing New Buildings.* Kaya Production, 1997

»Where The Stains Begin«. Bild/Text Kollaboration mit / Image/text collaboration with Lawrence Chua for *The Passionate Camera: Photography and Bodies of Desire*, New York, 1998

»Quod Nomen Mihi Est: Fragments from a Conversation with Satan«, *Felix: A Journal of Media Arts and Communication*, Vol. 2, no. 2, 1999.

* nicht in Düsseldorf ausgestellt /
not on view in Düsseldorf

SELF-PORTRAIT AS A FOUNTAIN, 2000
Videoskulptur / Video sculpture
183 x 549 x 305 cm
Kunstsammlung Nordrhein-Westfalen, Düsseldorf
Abb. Seite / ill. page 58-61

CARYATID, 2000*
Digitaler Videoloop, verchromter Monitor, DVD Spieler / digital video loop, chromed monitor, DVD Player
Monitorgröße / Monitor size:
25,4 x 30,5 x 30,5 cm
Bildgröße / image size: 15,2 x 19 cm
Abb. Seite / ill. page 42-43

24 LANDSCAPES, 2000
24 digitale Farbfotografien /
24 digital Cibachrome Prints
je / each: 40,7 x 51 cm
Thomas Dane, London
Abb. Seite / ill. page 4-11

THE FOUR HORSEMEN OF THE APOKALYPSE # 1, 2000*
Digital duraflex Print
152,5 x 122 cm
Abb. Seite / ill. page 34

THE FOUR HORSEMEN OF THE APOKALYPSE # 2, 2000*
Digital duraflex Print
152,5 x 122 cm
Abb. Seite / ill. page 35

THE FOUR HORSEMEN OF THE APOKALYPSE # 3, 2000*
Digital duraflex Print
152,5 x 122 cm
Abb. Seite / ill. page 37

THE FOUR HORSEMEN OF THE APOKALYPSE # 4, 2000*
Digital duraflex Print
152,5 x 122 cm
Abb. Seite / ill. page 30

THE LONG COUNT (I SHOOK UP THE WORLD), 2000/2001
digitaler Videoloop, LCD Monitor, DVD Spieler, Metallbefestigung /
Digital video loop, LCD monitor, DVD player, and metal armature
15,2 x 17,8 x 152,4 cm
schwarz-weiß, ohne Ton /
black and white, no sound
3' Loop
Sammlung Goetz
Abb. Seite / ill. page 52-53

THE LONG COUNT (RUMBLE IN THE JUNGLE), 2000/2001
digitaler Videoloop, LCD Monitor, DVD Spieler, Metallbefestigung /
Digital video loop, LCD monitor, DVD player, and metal armature
15,2 x 17,8 x 152,4 cm
Farbe, ohne Ton / color, no sound
3' Loop
Sammlung Goetz
Abb. Seite / ill. page 50-51

THE LONG COUNT (THRILLA IN MANILA), 2000/2001
digitaler Videoloop, LCD Monitor, DVD Spieler, Metallbefestigung /
Digital video loop, LCD monitor, DVD player, and metal armature
15,2 x 17,8 x 152,4 cm
Farbe / color 3' Loop
Privatsammlung / private collection
Courtesy White Cube, London
Abb. Seite / ill. page 54-55

ORPHEUS DESCENDING, 2000/2001
1.800 Stunden Filmmaterial /
1.800 hour Film
Projektionsdauer 75 Tage bei ununterbrochener Abspielzeit /
75 days of uninterrupted screening
Paul Pfeiffer, New York
Courtesy of The Project, New York and Los Angeles
Abb. Seite / ill. page 38-39

DUTCH INTERIOR, 2001
in die Wand eingelassenes Diorama, Peep-Loch, Videoprojektion /
Wall-recessed diorama, peephole, and live video feed
Dimensionen variabel /
Dimensions variable
Sammlung Goetz
Abb. Seite / ill. page 56-57

THE FOUR HORSEMEN OF THE APOKALYPSE # 5, 2001*
Digital duraflex Print
152,5 x 122 cm
Abb. Seite / ill. page 32

THE FOUR HORSEMEN OF THE APOKALYPSE # 6, 2001*
Digital duraflex Print
152,5 x 122 cm
Abb. Seite / ill. page 33

THREE STUDIES OF FIGURES AT THE BASE OF A CRUCIFIXION, 2001
Drei digitale Videoloops, drei Videoprojektoren, drei DVD Spieler, Metallbefestigungen / Three digital video loops, three video projectors, three DVD players, and metal armatures
Insgesamt/ Overall: 51 x 63,5 x 38 cm
Projiziertes Bild / Projected image:
9 x 46 cm
Abb. Seite / ill. page 44-49

THE FOUR HORSEMEN OF THE APOKALYPSE # 7, 2002
Digital duraflex Print
121,9 x 152,4 cm / 48 x 60"
Paul Pfeiffer, New York
Courtesy of The Project, New York and Los Angeles
Abb. Seite / ill. page 28-29

THE FOUR HORSEMEN OF THE APOKALYPSE # 8, 2002*
Digital duraflex Print
152,5 x 122 cm / 60 x 48"
Abb. Seite / ill. page 31

MORNING AFTER THE DELUGE, 2003
Video auf/on DVD
Projektion 3:4; Größe variabel /
Projektion 3:4; size variable
carlier | gebauer, Berlin
Abb. Seite / ill. page 40-41

FOTONACHWEIS
PHOTO CREDITS

Für die Reproduktionsvorlagen der Werke von Paul Pfeiffer / reproductions of Paul Pfeiffer's work: Paul Pfeiffer, New York
Für die Reproduktionsvorlagen der Werke von Thomas Ruff / works by Thomas Ruff: Thomas Ruff, Düsseldorf
Porträtfoto Paul Pfeiffer / Portrait of Paul Pfeiffer (S. 13): Courtesy Art21 © Art21, Inc.
Installationsfotos *Self-Portrait as a Fountain* (S. 58-59 und S. 61): Achim Kukulies, Düsseldorf

Diese Publikation erscheint anlässlich der Ausstellung /
This catalogue is published in conjunction with the exhibition

Paul Pfeiffer

12. Juni bis 17. Oktober 2004 / June 12–October 17, 2004
K21 Kunstsammlung Nordrhein-Westfalen, Düsseldorf

K20 K21
Kunstsammlung Nordrhein-Westfalen

DIREKTOR UND VORSTAND DER STIFTUNG
Armin Zweite

GESCHÄFTSFÜHRER
Otmar Böhmer

K20-WISSENSCHAFTLICHE LEITERIN
Pia Müller-Tamm

K21-KÜNSTLERISCHER LEITER
Julian Heynen

BILDUNG UND KOMMUNIKATION
Julia Breithaupt

MARKETING UND PRESSE
Cornelia Heising
Sven Bergmann

TECHNISCHER LEITER
Bernd Schliephake

RESTAURIERUNG
Werner Müller

BIBLIOTHEK
Henry Vauth

INTERNE VERWALTUNG
Susen Schubert

SPONSORING
Detmar Westhoff

Ausstellung / Exhibition

KURATOR / CURATOR
Valeria Liebermann

ARCHITEKTUR / ARCHITECTURE
Bernd Schliephake
und Team

BELEUCHTUNG / LIGHTS
Wilfried Kirste

REGISTRAR
Birgid Pudney-Schmidt
Katharina Nettekoven

KONSERVATORISCHE BETREUUNG / CONSERVATION
Werner Müller
Anne Skaliks

Katalog / Catalogue

HERAUSGEBER / EDITOR
K21 Kunstsammlung Nordrhein-Westfalen, Düsseldorf

REDAKTION / EDITING
Valeria Liebermann

ÜBERSETZUNGEN / TRANSLATIONS
Nikolaus G. Schneider, Berlin
Shaun Whiteside, London

GRAFISCHE GESTALTUNG UND SATZ / GRAPHIC DESIGN AND TYPESETTING
Anna Wesek, Düsseldorf

SCHRIFT / TYPEFACE
FF Din, Conduit ITC

PAPIER / PAPER
Alegro Halbmatt 150 g/qm

GESAMTHERSTELLUNG / PRINTED BY
Dr. Cantz'sche Druckerei,
Ostfildern-Ruit

Es erscheint eine Vorzugsausgabe mit 30 signierten und nummerierten C-Prints sowie 5 Epreuves d'artiste; nähere Informationen erhalten Sie beim Verlag. / A special collector's edition with 30 signed and numbered C-prints plus 5 artist's proofs is available; please contact Hatje Cantz for more information.

ERSCHIENEN IM / PUBLISHED BY
Hatje Cantz Verlag
Senefelderstraße 12
73760 Ostfildern-Ruit
Deutschland / Germany
Tel. +49 / 7 11 / 4 40 50
Fax +49 / 7 11 / 4 40 52 20
www.hatjecantz.com

Hatje Cantz books are available internationally at selected bookstores and from the following distribution partners:

USA/North America – D.A.P., Distributed Art Publishers, New York, www.artbook.com
UK – Art Books International, London, sales@art-bks.com
Australia – Towerbooks, French Forest (Sydney), towerbks@zipworld.com.au
France – Interart, Paris, interart.paris@wanadoo.fr
Belgium – Exhibitions International, Leuven, www.exhibitionsinternational.be

For Asia, Japan, South America, and Africa, as well as for general questions, please contact Hatje Cantz directly at sales@hatjecantz.de, or visit our homepage www.hatjecantz.com for further information.

ISBN 3-7757-1545-2
Printed in Germany

UMSCHLAGABBILDUNG / COVER ILLUSTRATION
24 Landscapes, 2000

FRONTISPIZ / FRONTISPIECE
Four Horsemen of the Apocalypse #1, 2000